CHALLENGE YOUR OCD!

A CBT Workbook for Young People with ASD

AMITA JASSI

Illustrated by Lisa Jo Robinson

Jessica Kingsley Publishers
London and Philadelphia

First published in Great Britain in 2021 by Jessica Kingsley Publishers
An Hachette Company

1

Copyright © Amita Jassi 2021
Illustrations copyright © Lisa Jo Robinson 2021

A CIP catalogue record for this title is available from the British Library and the Library of Congress

ISBN 978 1 78775 286 3
eISBN 978 1 78775 287 0

Printed and bound in Great Britain by Ashford Colour Ltd

Jessica Kingsley Publishers' policy is to use papers that are natural, renewable and recyclable products and made from wood grown in sustainable forests. The logging and manufacturing processes are expected to conform to the environmental regulations of the country of origin.

Jessica Kingsley Publishers
73 Collier Street
London N1 9BE, UK

www.jkp.com

Contents

Acknowledgements 9

**SESSION 1: INTRODUCTION AND
LEARNING ABOUT OCD** 11
SESSION 1 PLAN 12
LEARNING ABOUT CBT FOR OCD 13
GETTING TO KNOW YOU 14
WHAT IS OCD? 15
WHAT CAUSES OCD? 16
OCD IS NOT YOU! 17
HOMEWORK SESSION 1 18

**SESSION 2: LEARNING ABOUT
ASD AND OCD** 19
SESSION 2 PLAN 20
RECAP: SESSION 1 21
WHAT IS ASD? 22
DIFFERENCES BETWEEN OCD AND ASD 24
HOMEWORK SESSION 2 25

SESSION 3: LEARNING ABOUT ANXIETY 27
SESSION 3 PLAN 28
RECAP: SESSION 2 29
WHAT IS ANXIETY? 30
WHY DO WE GET ANXIOUS? 31
ANXIETY RATING SCALE 32
YOUR ANXIETY RATING SCALE 33
HOMEWORK SESSION 3 34
HOMEWORK: YOUR OCD DIARY 35
HOMEWORK: OCD DIARY FOR FAMILY 36

**SESSION 4: LEARNING ABOUT
ANXIETY AND OCD** 37
SESSION 4 PLAN 38
RECAP: SESSION 3 39
ANXIETY HABITUATION 40
THE OCD CYCLE 42
YOUR OCD CYCLE 43
WHAT HAPPENS TO ANXIETY IN OCD? 44
HOW TO BREAK THE OCD CYCLE 45
ANXIETY HABITUATION WHEN BREAKING
THE OCD CYCLE 46
HOMEWORK SESSION 4 47
HOMEWORK: YOUR OCD CYCLE 48
HOMEWORK: YOUR OCD DIARY 50
HOMEWORK: OCD DIARY FOR FAMILY 51

SESSION 5: SETTING UP A PLAN 53
SESSION 5 PLAN 54
RECAP: SESSION 4 55
WHAT IS ERP? 56
OCD HIERARCHY 57
OCD HIERARCHY: AVOIDANCE 59
OCD HIERARCHY: WHAT OTHER PEOPLE
DO FOR OCD 60
GOALS 61
HOMEWORK SESSION 5 62
HOMEWORK: PUT OCD IN ORDER 63

SESSION 6: CHALLENGING OCD USING ERP . 67
SESSION 6 PLAN 68
RECAP: SESSION 5 69
CBT FOR OCD QUIZ! 70
FIRST ERP TASK! 71
HOMEWORK SESSION 6 73
HOMEWORK: ERP TASKS! TIMETABLE 74
HOMEWORK: ERP TASKS! 75

SESSION 7: CHALLENGING OCD USING ERP (AND OCD REVIEW) 77

SESSION 7 PLAN   78

RECAP: SESSION 6   79

REVIEW OCD   80

ERP TASK!   81

HOMEWORK SESSION 7   83

HOMEWORK: ERP TASKS!   84

SESSION 8: CHALLENGING OCD USING ERP .   85

SESSION 8 PLAN   86

RECAP: SESSION 7   87

ERP TASK!   88

OCD STEPS   90

HOMEWORK SESSION 8   91

HOMEWORK: ERP TASKS!   92

SESSION 9: CHALLENGING OCD USING ERP .   93

SESSION 9 PLAN   94

RECAP: SESSION 8   95

ERP TASK!   96

OCD STEPS (OPTIONAL)   98

THINGS TO HELP YOU DO ERP   99

HOMEWORK SESSION 9   100

HOMEWORK: ERP TASKS!   101

HOMEWORK: OCD STEPS (OPTIONAL)   102

SESSION 10: CHALLENGING OCD USING ERP   103

SESSION 10 PLAN   104

RECAP: SESSION 9   105

ERP TASK!   106

OCD STEPS (OPTIONAL)   109

HOMEWORK SESSION 10   110

HOMEWORK: ERP TASKS!   111

SESSION 11: CHALLENGING OCD USING ERP   113

SESSION 11 PLAN   114

RECAP: SESSION 10   115

ERP TASK!   116

OCD STEPS (OPTIONAL)   119

HOMEWORK SESSION 11   120

HOMEWORK: ERP TASKS!   121

SESSION 12: CHALLENGING OCD USING ERP   123

SESSION 12 PLAN   124

RECAP: SESSION 11   125

ERP TASK!   126

RULES FOR CHALLENGING OCD   129

OCD STEPS (OPTIONAL)   130

HOMEWORK SESSION 12   131

HOMEWORK: ERP TASKS!   132

SESSION 13: CHALLENGING OCD USING ERP   135

SESSION 13 PLAN   136

RECAP: SESSION 12   137

ERP TASK!   138

OCD STEPS (OPTIONAL)   141

HOMEWORK SESSION 13   142

HOMEWORK: ERP TASKS!   143

SESSION 14: CHALLENGING OCD USING ERP (AND OCD REVIEW) 145

SESSION 14 PLAN   146

RECAP: SESSION 13   147

REVIEW OCD   148

ERP TASK!   149

OCD STEPS (OPTIONAL)   152

HOMEWORK SESSION 14   153

HOMEWORK: ERP TASKS!   154

HOMEWORK: RE-RATE YOUR HIERARCHY   156

SESSION 15: CHALLENGING OCD USING ERP – YOU TAKE CHARGE 161

SESSION 15 PLAN   162

RECAP: SESSION 14   163

ERP TASK!   164

OCD STEPS (OPTIONAL)   167

THINGS TO HELP YOU DO ERP   168

HOMEWORK SESSION 15   169

HOMEWORK: ERP TASKS!   170

SESSION 16: CHALLENGING OCD USING ERP – YOU TAKE CHARGE 173

SESSION 16 PLAN   174
RECAP: SESSION 15   175
ERP TASK!   176
OCD STEPS (OPTIONAL)   179
HOMEWORK SESSION 16   180
HOMEWORK: ERP TASKS!   181

SESSION 17: CHALLENGING OCD USING ERP – YOU TAKE CHARGE 183

SESSION 17 PLAN   184
RECAP: SESSION 16   185
ERP TASK!   186
OCD STEPS (OPTIONAL)   189
HOMEWORK SESSION 17   190
HOMEWORK: ERP TASKS!   191

SESSION 18: CHALLENGING OCD USING ERP – YOU TAKE CHARGE 193

SESSION 18 PLAN   194
RECAP: SESSION 17   195
ERP TASK!   196
OCD STEPS (OPTIONAL)   199
HOMEWORK SESSION 18   200
HOMEWORK: ERP TASKS!   201

SESSION 19: CHALLENGING OCD USING ERP AND GETTING READY FOR THE FINISH .. 203

SESSION 19 PLAN   204
RECAP: SESSION 18   205
ERP OR EXTREME TASK!   206
GETTING READY FOR THE FINISH   209
OCD STEPS (OPTIONAL)   210
HOMEWORK SESSION 19   211
HOMEWORK: ERP TASKS!   212

SESSION 20: RELAPSE PREVENTION PLAN ... 215

SESSION 20 PLAN   216
RECAP: SESSION 19   217
RELAPSE PREVENTION PLAN   218
REVIEW OCD   220
PLANNING AHEAD   221
OCD STEPS (OPTIONAL)   222

APPENDIX: THINGS TO HELP YOU IN TREATMENT 225

DIFFERENT FEELINGS   226
LEARNING ABOUT THOUGHTS   227
HELPFUL THOUGHTS   229
ASK OTHERS TO CHALLENGE OCD   231
DO A SURVEY OR FIND OUT FACTS   233
EXTREME TASKS   235

FOLLOW-UP 1: REVIEW PROGRESS AND PLAN 237

FOLLOW-UP 1 PLAN   238
REVIEW AND PLAN   239
REVIEW AND MEASURE OCD (OPTIONAL)   240

FOLLOW-UP 2: REVIEW PROGRESS AND PLAN 241

FOLLOW-UP 2 PLAN   242
REVIEW AND PLAN   243
REVIEW AND MEASURE OCD   244

FOLLOW-UP 3: REVIEW PROGRESS AND PLAN 245

FOLLOW-UP 3 PLAN   246
REVIEW AND PLAN   247
REVIEW AND MEASURE OCD   248

FOLLOW-UP 4: REVIEW PROGRESS AND PLAN 249

FOLLOW-UP 4 PLAN   250
REVIEW AND PLAN   251
REVIEW AND MEASURE OCD   252
LOOKING TO THE FUTURE   253

Acknowledgements

I would like to thank my colleagues (both past and present) at the National and Specialist OCD, BDD and Related Disorders Team for Young People, South London and Maudsley NHS Trust, UK. There are too many to mention but they have each contributed to the development of this treatment in different ways. In particular, I wish to thank Victoria Hallett, Gazal Jones, Zoe Kindynis, Benedetta Monzani, Lauren Peile and Kelly Wood for their helpful contributions. Thank you to Olivia Brooks-Wilkins who assisted with the illustration development of the OCD character used in this workbook.

I wish to acknowledge the two fantastic OCD treatment manuals available that have helped shape this workbook. These are *OCD and Autism: A Clinician's Guide to Adapting CBT* by Ailsa Russell, Amita Jassi and Kate Johnston and *OCD – Tools to Help You Fight Back! A CBT Workbook for Young People* by Cynthia Turner, Georgina Krebs and Chloe Volz. Thank you to Georgina Krebs and Ailsa Russell for supporting the development and evaluation of this treatment for young people with ASD.

I wish to thank South London and Maudsley NHS Trust for the space and time to develop and trial this treatment, and the Biomedical Research Council for providing funding for the development of this workbook.

Finally, I wish to express my gratitude to all the young people and families I have had the privilege to work with over the years. This has given me incredible insight into their experiences, which has helped to develop this treatment. I hope it will benefit many more people out there.

SESSION 1

INTRODUCTION
AND LEARNING
ABOUT OCD

SESSION 1 PLAN

- Learning about CBT for OCD ☐

- Getting to know you ☐

- What is OCD? ☐

- What causes OCD? ☐

- Set homework ☐

- Anything you want to add to the agenda? ☐

. . . .

. . . .

. . . .

. . . .

. . . .

. . . .

INTRODUCTION AND LEARNING ABOUT OCD

LEARNING ABOUT CBT FOR OCD

CBT stands for cognitive behaviour therapy. You will be offered up to 20 sessions of CBT and ideally you should have a session every week.

CBT for OCD involves working with your therapist and family to challenge OCD step by step. Below is an outline of what you will cover in sessions – treatment works best if you follow the plan below.

Sessions 1–4	The education phase of treatment is where you and your family will learn about OCD and how it works. You will discuss autism spectrum disorder (ASD) too, and spend time learning about anxiety as this is an important part of OCD.
Sessions 5–6	Develop a hierarchy (list of things OCD makes you/others do or avoid) and use this to plan exposure and response prevention (ERP) tasks. ERP is where you face a situation that triggers your OCD and then resist doing what OCD wants you (or other people) to do. You will give this a try in Session 6.
Session 7	Review your OCD and do an ERP task.
Sessions 8–13	Do regular ERP tasks and learn some things to help you do these tasks.
Session 14	Review your OCD and do an ERP task.
Sessions 15–19	Continue to do regular ERP tasks and learn some things to help you do these tasks. You will start to take charge of tasks from this point.
Session 20	Relapse prevention is important – this is where you come up with a plan to make sure OCD does not come back.
Follow-up appointments	After your regular treatment sessions end, you will be offered four follow-up sessions over 12 months to help you keep OCD away.

You and your family will be given tasks to do between each session. These tasks are super important and have been found to help people get better from OCD!

GETTING TO KNOW YOU

Who is in your family?

. . . .

. . . .

. . . .

. . . .

Do you go to school or college? If so, what are your favourite classes?

. . . .

. . . .

. . . .

. . . .

If not, what do you do during the day?

. . . .

. . . .

What are your interests and favourite activities?

. . . .

. . . .

. . . .

. . . .

Is there anything else you want to tell us about you?

. . . .

. . . .

. . . .

. . . .

WHAT IS OCD?

- OCD stands for obsessive compulsive disorder.

- O is for obsessions – these are unwanted thoughts, worries, pictures, urges or doubts that come into our minds.

- C is for compulsions – these are actions or behaviours we do, sometimes to make the obsession go away, to reduce uncomfortable feelings or just because OCD makes us feel we have to do them. You can see some compulsions, others are done in our head and sometimes other people have to do compulsions for OCD too.

- D is for disorder – this means obsessions and compulsions are annoying, distressing and get in the way of what we really want to be doing.

- Did you know that OCD is very common? Around one to two in every 100 young people have OCD!

Here are some common obsessions and compulsions – tick the ones that apply to you and add some that are not on the list.

Some common obsessions are:
- ☐ fears about contamination or getting ill
- ☐ worries about something bad happening to you or someone else
- ☐ unwanted sexual thoughts
- ☐ worries about offending God.

Can you add more?

....

....

Some common compulsions are:
- ☐ washing and cleaning
- ☐ checking
- ☐ reassurance seeking
- ☐ repeating rituals.

Can you add more?

....

....

15

WHAT CAUSES OCD?

- We do not know the cause of OCD.
- We know that it is no one's fault you have OCD.
- Some research has shown the following may make you more likely to develop OCD:
    - Imbalance of serotonin in the brain.
    - Family members having OCD or other related difficulties.
    - Stresses in your life.
    - Having an anxious personality.
- Even though we do not know what causes OCD, we know how people can get better!

OCD IS NOT YOU!

It is important to remember OCD is not part of you – it is like a bully that makes you experience obsessions and do compulsions.

Would you like to draw what you think OCD looks like? You may prefer to name OCD, or you can write some words to describe it. This is to help make you feel separate from your OCD.

HOMEWORK SESSION 1

- Read over Session 1. ☐
- Write three things you learned or remember from Session 1: ☐

....

....

....

....

....

- Finish drawing, naming or describing OCD. ☐
- Watch some videos on OCD. ☐
- Other homework: ☐

....

....

....

....

....

- Write down questions you or your family have for the next session: ☐

....

....

....

....

....

18

SESSION 2

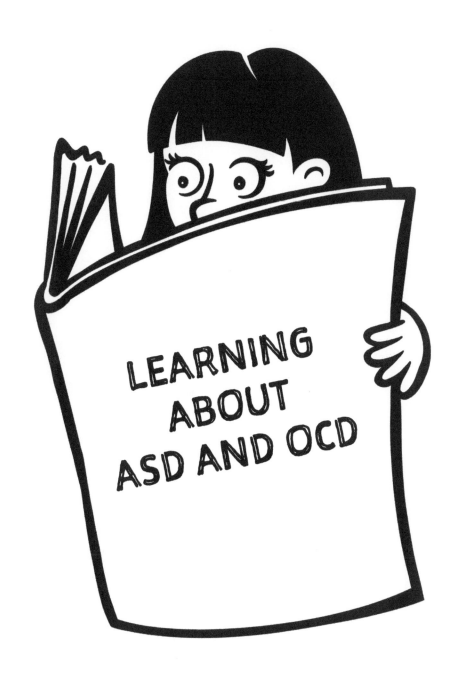

LEARNING
ABOUT
ASD AND OCD

SESSION 2 PLAN

- Recap of Session 1 ☐

- Homework review ☐

- What is ASD? ☐

- Differences between OCD and ASD ☐

- Set homework ☐

- Anything you want to add to the agenda? ☐

. . . .

. . . .

. . . .

. . . .

. . . .

. . . .

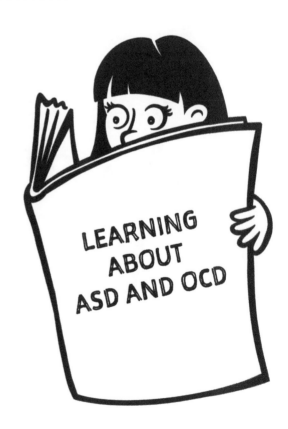

RECAP: SESSION 1

In Session 1, we learned about:

● you, your interests and your family

● what OCD is

● what we know about the causes of OCD.

Now let's look over your homework.

WHAT IS ASD?

- ASD stands for autism spectrum disorder.
- ASD affects how the brain and body work and it affects people in different ways.
- In particular, it can impact on social interaction, communication, interests and behaviours.
- We do not know the cause of ASD.
- Around one in 100 people have ASD.

 Look at the boxes below, tick what you think applies to you and add more information:

SOCIAL INTERACTION

- Enjoy own company. ☐
- Difficulties understanding other people's facial expressions. ☐
- Eye contact can be difficult at times. ☐

....
....
....
....
....
....

COMMUNICATION

- Prefer to say things clearly and straight to the point. ☐
- Enjoy talking about special interests. ☐

....
....
....
....
....
....

INTERESTS

- Strong interests in particular things (special interests). ☐
- Enjoy doing the same or similar activities over and over. ☐

....
....
....
....
....
....

BEHAVIOURS

- Like activities that are structured and predictable. ☐
- Prefer particular routines. ☐

....
....
....
....
....
....

OTHER

- Dislike particular sounds, smells, touch of things, taste or look of things. ☐

....
....
....
....
....
....

DIFFERENCES BETWEEN OCD AND ASD

There are parts of OCD and ASD that may appear similar, but there are also important differences. This treatment focuses on challenging OCD, so it is important to be clear about what you will be working on.

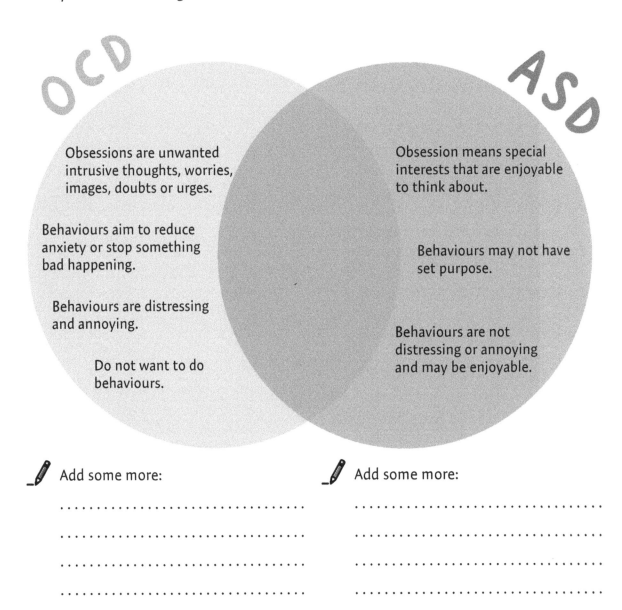

OCD

Obsessions are unwanted intrusive thoughts, worries, images, doubts or urges.

Behaviours aim to reduce anxiety or stop something bad happening.

Behaviours are distressing and annoying.

Do not want to do behaviours.

ASD

Obsession means special interests that are enjoyable to think about.

Behaviours may not have set purpose.

Behaviours are not distressing or annoying and may be enjoyable.

Add some more:

. . . .

. . . .

. . . .

. . . .

Add some more:

. . . .

. . . .

. . . .

. . . .

Would you like to find out more about thoughts? If so, see the Appendix: Learning about Thoughts.

HOMEWORK SESSION 2

- Read over Session 2. ☐
- Write three things you learned or remember from Session 2: ☐

. . . .

. . . .

. . . .

. . . .

- Watch an animation on ASD. ☐
- Add other things you know about ASD. ☐
- Other homework: ☐

. . . .

. . . .

. . . .

. . . .

- Write down questions you or your family have for the next session: ☐

. . . .

. . . .

. . . .

. . . .

LEARNING ABOUT ASD AND OCD

SESSION 3

SESSION 3 PLAN

- Recap of Session 2 □

- Homework review □

- What is anxiety? □

- Why do we get anxious? □

- Anxiety rating scale □

- Set homework □

- Anything you want to add to the agenda? □

....

....

....

....

....

LEARNING ABOUT ANXIETY

RECAP: SESSION 2

In Session 2, we learned about:

● what ASD is

● some of the characteristics of ASD that you may have

● the differences between OCD and ASD.

Now let's look over your homework.

WHAT IS ANXIETY?

Anxiety is a normal feeling that everyone experiences (including animals). When we get anxious, we get physical sensations in our bodies that give us a clue that we are feeling anxious.

Think about the last time you felt anxious, what did you notice in your body? Tick the ones that apply to you and add some more.

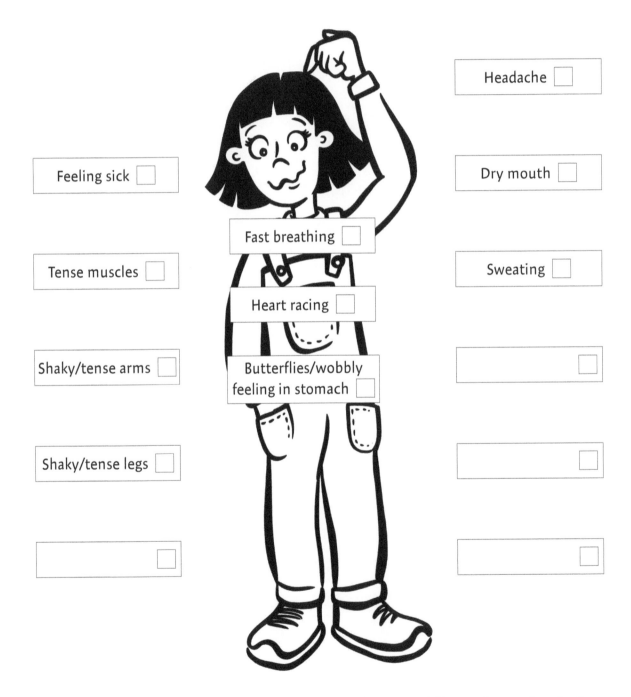

Headache ☐

Feeling sick ☐

Dry mouth ☐

Fast breathing ☐

Tense muscles ☐

Sweating ☐

Heart racing ☐

Shaky/tense arms ☐

Butterflies/wobbly feeling in stomach ☐

☐

Shaky/tense legs ☐

☐

☐

☐

If you are finding it tricky to recognize anxiety and how it is different from other feelings, see Appendix: Different Feelings.

WHY DO WE GET ANXIOUS?

- Anxiety symptoms get triggered when we think we are in danger.
- This is known as the fight or flight response.
- Sometimes we need this response to be triggered and sometimes we do not.
- Can you think of times when it is helpful?

. . . .

. . . .

. . . .

. . . .

- Can you think of examples when it is not helpful?

. . . .

. . . .

. . . .

. . . .

ANXIETY RATING SCALE

- Anxiety comes at different levels.
- Some situations or things can make us a little bit anxious, while others can make us really anxious. Some things can make us feel somewhere in-between.
- In this treatment, we need to measure different levels of anxiety; there are examples of how to do this below.

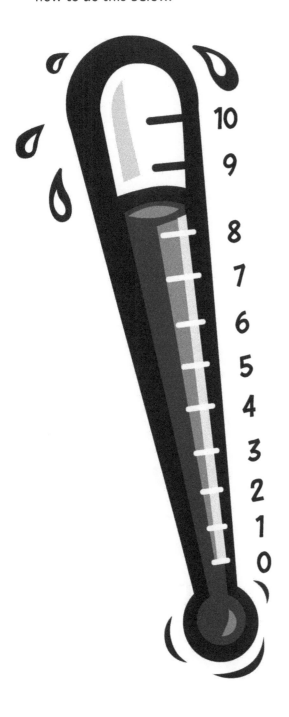

YOUR ANXIETY RATING SCALE

✎ Now it is time to come up with your anxiety rating scale. You can pick one from the previous page or draw your own.

✎ Let's write some examples of different things or situations that make you anxious on your scale. Try to think of non-OCD examples.

HOMEWORK SESSION 3

- Read over Session 3. ☐
- Write three things you learned or remember from Session 3: ☐

....

....

....

....

- Add any physical signs of anxiety you notice between now and the next session. ☐
- Complete your anxiety rating scale and practise using your scale. ☐
- Keep a diary of OCD symptoms this week. There is also a diary for your family to complete. ☐
- Other homework: ☐

....

....

....

....

- Write down questions you or your family have for the next session: ☐

....

....

....

....

LEARNING ABOUT ANXIETY

HOMEWORK: YOUR OCD DIARY

An important part of challenging OCD is to keep track of it. Use the diary below to write down any time you notice OCD around this week.

Date	What did OCD make you or others do or avoid?	How long did you have to do it or how many times did you have to do it?

HOMEWORK: OCD DIARY FOR FAMILY

An important part of challenging OCD is to keep track of it. It is useful for your family to do this too. Use the diary below to write down any time you notice OCD around this week.

Date	What OCD symptom did you notice? (Compulsion, avoidance or something you or someone else did?)	How long or how many times?

SESSION 4

LEARNING
ABOUT
ANXIETY AND
OCD

SESSION 4 PLAN

- Recap of Session 3 ☐

- Homework review ☐

- Anxiety habituation ☐

- The OCD cycle ☐

- What happens to anxiety in OCD? ☐

- How to break the OCD cycle ☐

- Anxiety habituation when breaking the OCD cycle ☐

- Set homework ☐

- Anything you want to add to the agenda? ☐

. . . .

. . . .

. . . .

. . . .

. . . .

LEARNING ABOUT ANXIETY AND OCD

RECAP: SESSION 3

In Session 3, we learned about:

● anxiety

● fight or flight response

● anxiety rating scale.

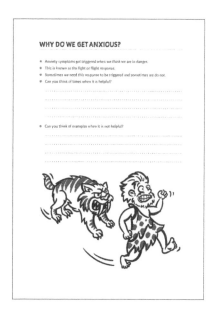

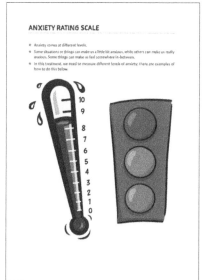

Now let's look over your homework.

ANXIETY HABITUATION

Anxiety habituation describes what happens to anxiety if you face something that makes you feel anxious, you stay in the situation and do not do anything to reduce your anxiety.

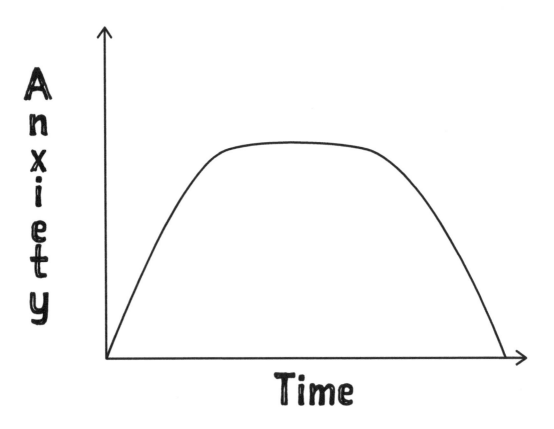

At first, anxiety increases, and it can feel like this happens really quickly.

Anxiety peaks but it does not rise anymore and usually stays at the same level.

If you stay in the situation, then anxiety starts to reduce and eventually comes down.

What happens to anxiety if you face a scary situation or thing over and over again?

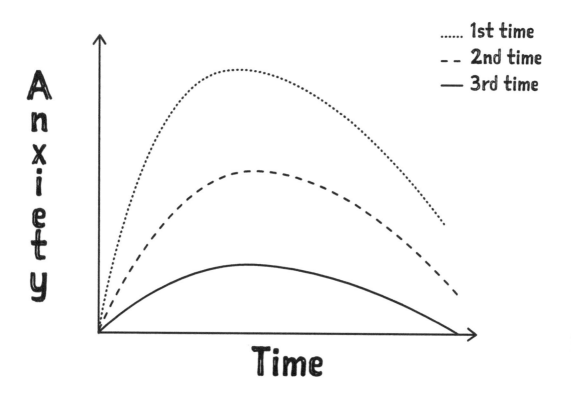

First time – anxiety goes up high, but it eventually comes back down.

Second time – anxiety goes up, but not as high as the first time and comes back down.

Third time – anxiety rises, but not as high as the second time and again it comes back down.

What do you think would happen on the fourth, fifth, sixth time?

. . . .

. . . .

. . . .

. . . .

. . . .

. . . .

THE OCD CYCLE

Let's have a look at how OCD works.

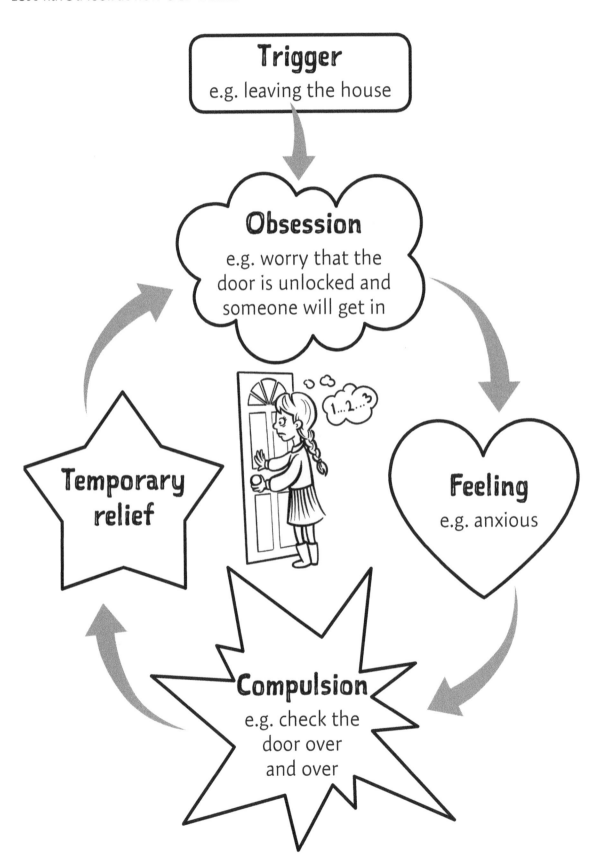

YOUR OCD CYCLE

✏️ Use this page to think of an example of how your OCD works.

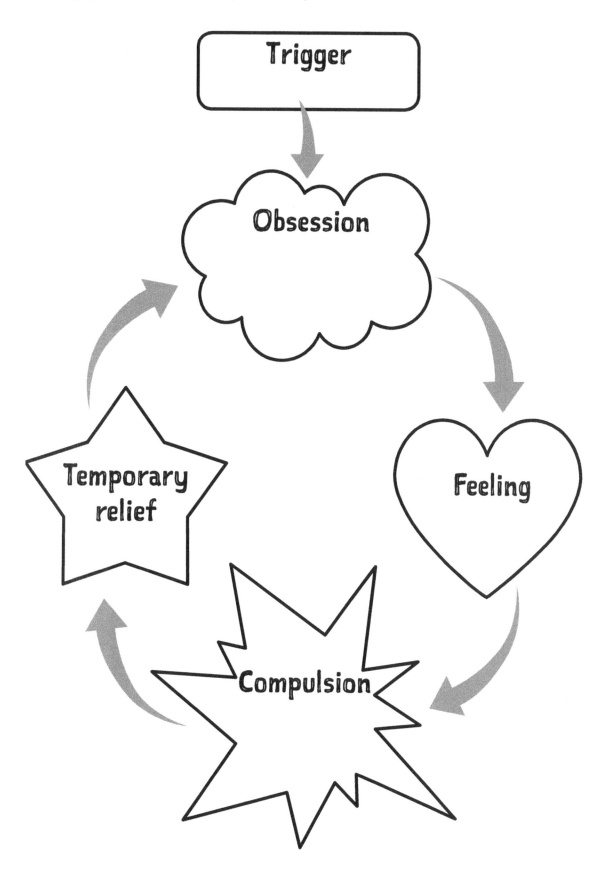

WHAT HAPPENS TO ANXIETY IN OCD?

- We have learned that when you do a compulsion, you get temporary relief from your anxiety.

- When you do a compulsion, the anxiety you feel is brought down quickly.

- This seems like a good idea at the time, but OCD will make your anxiety go up to the same level or higher each time and will keep asking you to do more and more compulsions.

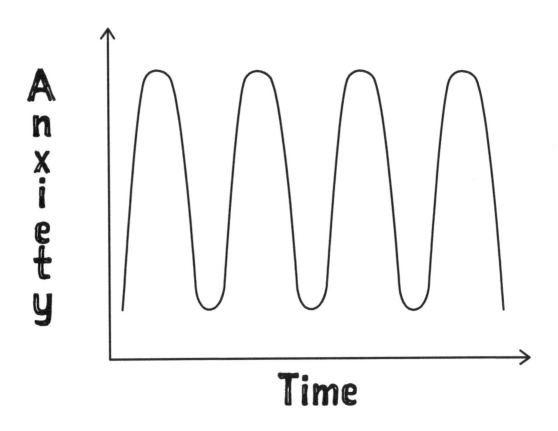

Let's turn to the next page to see how we can tackle OCD.

HOW TO BREAK THE OCD CYCLE

Let's look at how to break the OCD cycle.

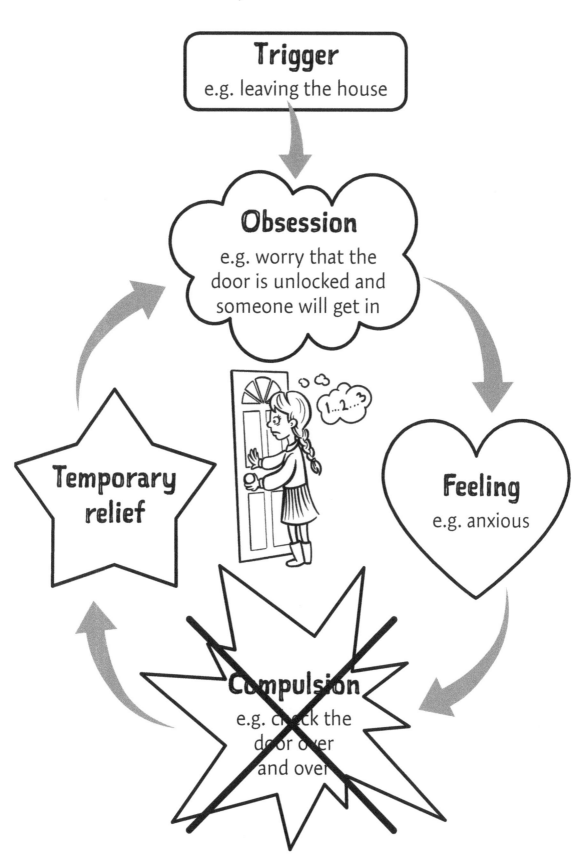

ANXIETY HABITUATION WHEN BREAKING THE OCD CYCLE

Remember what happens to anxiety if you keep facing a scary situation or thing over and over again? The same thing happens when you do not do a compulsion.

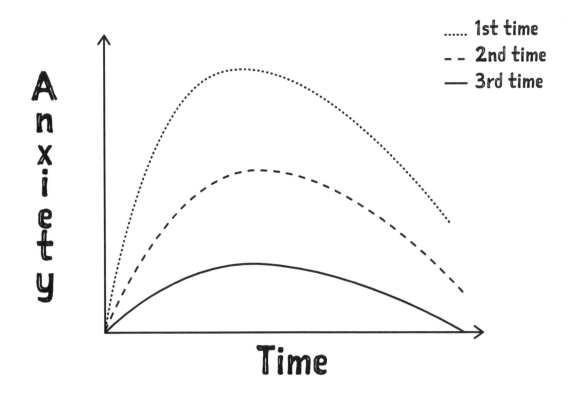

First time – when you resist doing a compulsion, your anxiety will go up high, but it will eventually come back down.

Second time – anxiety will go up when you resist the same compulsion, but not as high as the first time and it will come back down.

Third time – anxiety will rise when you resist the same compulsion, but not as high as the second time and again it will come back down.

If you continue to resist the compulsion over and over again, your anxiety will reduce each time and it will get easier and easier to challenge OCD.

HOMEWORK SESSION 4

- Read over Session 4. ☐
- Write three things you learned or remember from Session 4: ☐

  ....

  ....

  ....

  ....

- Complete OCD cycles. ☐
- Keep a diary of OCD symptoms this week. There is also a diary for
  your family to complete. ☐
- Other homework: ☐

  ....

  ....

  ....

  ....

- Write down questions you or your family have for the next session: ☐

  ....

  ....

  ....

  ....

HOMEWORK: YOUR OCD CYCLE

🖊 Use this page to think of an example of how your OCD works.

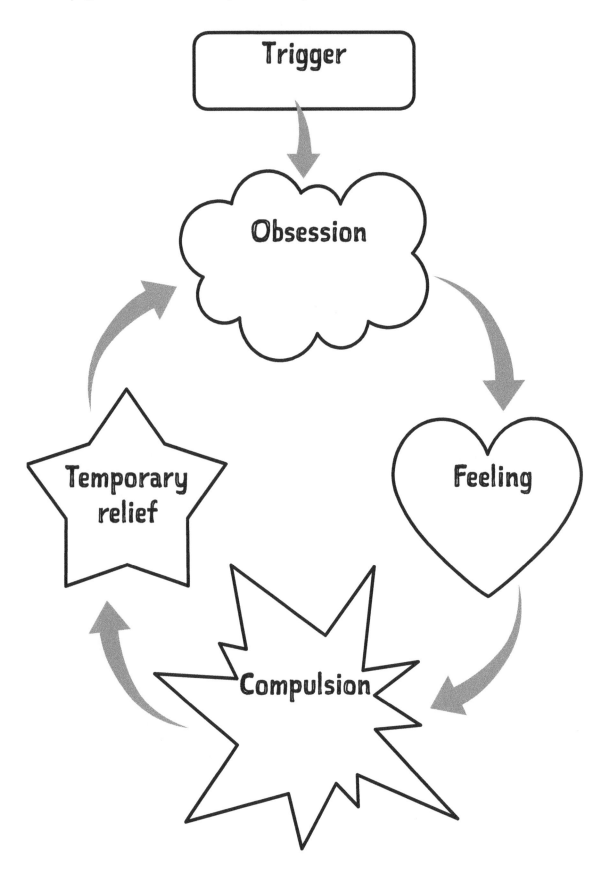

HOMEWORK: YOUR OCD CYCLE

🖊 Use this page to think of an example of how your OCD works.

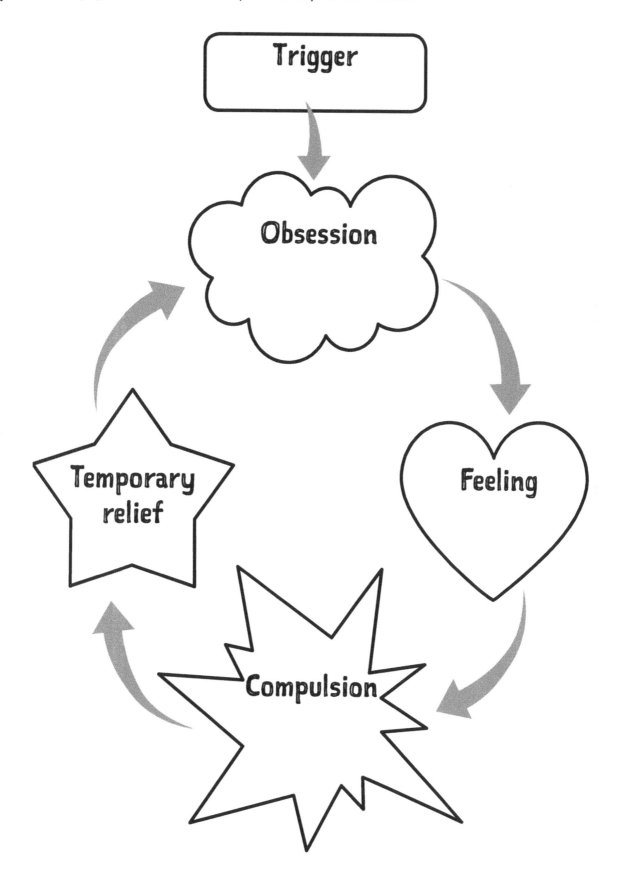

HOMEWORK: YOUR OCD DIARY

An important part of challenging OCD is to keep track of it. Use the diary below to write down any time you notice OCD around this week.

Date	What did OCD make you or others do or avoid?	How long did you have to do it or how many times did you have to do it?

HOMEWORK: OCD DIARY FOR FAMILY

An important part of challenging OCD is to keep track of it. It is useful for your family to do this too. They can use the diary below to write down any time they notice OCD around this week.

Date	What OCD symptom did you notice? (Compulsion, avoidance or something you or someone else did?)	How long or how many times?

SESSION 5

SETTING
UP A PLAN

SESSION 5 PLAN

- Recap of Session 4 ☐

- Homework review ☐

- What is ERP? ☐

- OCD hierarchy ☐

- Goals ☐

- Set homework ☐

- Anything you want to add to the agenda? ☐

. . . .

. . . .

. . . .

. . . .

. . . .

SETTING UP A PLAN

RECAP: SESSION 4

In Session 4, we learned about:

- anxiety habituation
- the OCD cycle
- what happens to anxiety in OCD
- how to break the OCD cycle
- anxiety habituation when breaking the OCD cycle.

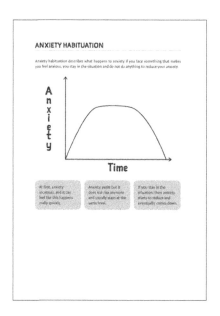

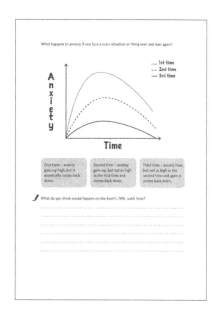

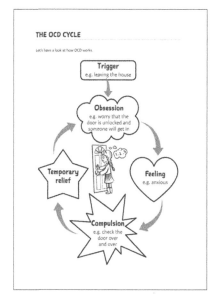

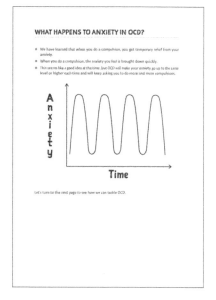

Now let's look over your homework.

WHAT IS ERP?

- ERP stands for exposure and response prevention.
- This is the most important part of treatment for OCD.
- Exposure means facing a situation which triggers your OCD.
- Response prevention means not doing what OCD wants you or other people to do.
- To help you do ERP, we need a plan. The plan we will use in treatment is called a hierarchy.

OCD HIERARCHY

This is important to use when you plan to challenge OCD. It is a list of all the things OCD makes you do and avoid, and the things it makes others do. Once you have your list, use your anxiety rating scale from Session 3 to write how anxious you would feel if you or others did not listen to OCD. You can use the diaries you and your family completed to help you.

Let's give it a go, starting with what OCD makes you do.

Compulsion (What OCD makes you do)	Anxiety rating (If you did not do the compulsion)

Compulsion (What OCD makes you do)	Anxiety rating (If you did not do the compulsion)

OCD HIERARCHY: AVOIDANCE

Now let's list things that OCD makes you avoid and rate how anxious you would feel if you did not avoid these things or situations.

What I avoid (What OCD stops you from doing)	Anxiety rating (If you did not avoid)

OCD HIERARCHY: WHAT OTHER PEOPLE DO FOR OCD

Let's all think about what others have to do for OCD – this can include anyone in your family, your friends, your teachers...anyone!

Make a list and rate how anxious you would feel if they did not do this.

What other people do (Things other people do or not do because of OCD)	Anxiety rating (If they did not do this)

GOALS

Let's think about what life would be like if OCD was not around anymore. What would you be able to do that you cannot do now? Let's list some goals – your therapist will help you with this.

By the middle of treatment, I would like to be able to:

....

....

....

To do this, I need to challenge the following OCD symptoms:

....

....

....

By the end of treatment, I would like to be able to:

....

....

....

To do this, I need to challenge the following OCD symptoms:

....

....

....

In a year from now, I would like to be able to:

....

....

....

To do this, I need to challenge the following OCD symptoms:

....

....

....

HOMEWORK SESSION 5

- Read over Session 5. ☐
- Write three things you learned or remember from Session 5: ☐

. . . .

. . . .

. . . .

. . . .

- Complete OCD hierarchies. ☐
- Finish your goals. ☐
- Put OCD in order. ☐
- Other homework: ☐

. . . .

. . . .

. . . .

. . . .

- Write down questions you or your family have for the next session: ☐

. . . .

. . . .

. . . .

. . . .

SETTING
UP A PLAN

62

HOMEWORK: PUT OCD IN ORDER

Using your lists of things OCD makes you and others do, and what it makes you avoid, please now put these things in order from what makes you feel the least anxious to what makes you feel the most.

Compulsion/Avoid/What others do	Anxiety rating

Compulsion/Avoid/What others do	Anxiety rating
64	

Compulsion/Avoid/What others do	Anxiety rating

Compulsion/Avoid/What others do	Anxiety rating
65	
Compulsion/Avoid/What others do	Anxiety rating

Compulsion/Avoid/What others do	Anxiety rating
66	

SESSION 6

CHALLENGING
OCD USING
ERP

SESSION 6 PLAN

- Recap of Session 5 ☐

- Homework review ☐

- CBT for OCD quiz! ☐

- First ERP task! ☐

- Set homework ☐

- Anything you want to add to the agenda? ☐

....

....

....

....

....

CHALLENGING OCD USING ERP

RECAP: SESSION 5

In Session 5, we learned about:

- ERP
- OCD hierarchies
- goals.

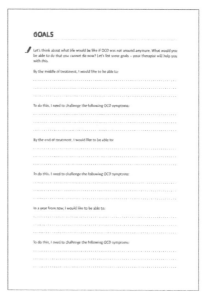

Now let's look over your homework.

CBT FOR OCD QUIZ!

You have learned a lot about OCD, ASD, anxiety and how to challenge OCD.

Let's do a true or false quiz to see how much you can remember.

- Anxiety can be a useful feeling that in some situations keeps us safe when we face danger.

  True ☐   False ☐

- Anxiety keeps rising and does not stop when you face something scary.

  True ☐   False ☐

- Anxiety comes down by itself when you face something scary and it gets less scary if you do it over and over again.

  True ☐   False ☐

- The OCD cycle explains how obsessions make us anxious and compulsions give us temporary relief.

  True ☐   False ☐

- ERP (exposure and response prevention) is when you keep doing what OCD wants you to do.

  True ☐   False ☐

- We use an OCD hierarchy to help plan ERP tasks, starting with easier tasks and working up to harder ones.

  True ☐   False ☐

FIRST ERP TASK!

It's time to start challenging OCD! This sheet gives you a step-by-step guide to setting up an ERP task. Let's look at your hierarchy from Session 5 to help us decide where to start. You will need your anxiety rating scale from Session 3.

STEP 1: Before we start, what level is your anxiety at the moment? Add this to the table on the next page in the column 'Before task'.

STEP 2: Pick one thing OCD makes you do or avoid or what others do from your OCD list.

. . . .

. . . .

STEP 3: What obsession does this relate to? (What is OCD telling you to worry about?)

. . . .

. . . .

STEP 4: What will the exposure be?

. . . .

. . . .

STEP 5: What will the response prevention be?

. . . .

. . . .

STEP 6: What level do you predict your anxiety will be?

. . . .

. . . .

STEP 7: Let's do the ERP task and fill out the table on the next page with your anxiety ratings. This is really important to see what happens to your anxiety over time.

STEP 8: End the task when anxiety is half of what it was at '0 mins' or when it is back to the 'Before task' level.

STEP 9: What did you learn about anxiety doing this task? Did you learn anything about your obsession?

. . . .

. . . .

Well done, you just did your first ERP task!

Challenge your OCD. Let's see what happens to your anxiety when you do this.

Date	ERP task!	Anxiety ratings					
		Before task	0 mins	5 mins	15 mins	30 mins	60 mins

You have measured your anxiety over one hour. Consider what happens to it after two, three, four hours, overnight or by the next day. For your task to be useful, keep recording your anxiety until it has come down at least by half (e.g. from 6 to 3) or it is back to what it was before you did the task.

HOMEWORK SESSION 6

- Read over Session 6. ☐
- Write three things you learned or remember from Session 6: ☐

  . . . .

  . . . .

  . . . .

  . . . .

- Keep adding to the hierarchies with any new compulsions, things you avoid or what others have to do for OCD you notice. ☐
- Practise the ERP task you did in the session (use the timetable on the next page to help you plan, and also keep track of your progress). ☐
- Other homework: ☐

  . . . .

  . . . .

  . . . .

  . . . .

- Write down questions you or your family have for the next session: ☐

  . . . .

  . . . .

  . . . .

  . . . .

CHALLENGING OCD USING ERP

HOMEWORK: ERP TASKS! TIMETABLE

Use the table below to plan when you will complete your ERP tasks, or you can create your own! It is important to practise them as much as possible – remember, the more you do them, the easier they will get!

Day	Time	ERP task(s)	Help needed?	Done √

HOMEWORK: ERP TASKS!

Challenge your OCD. Let's see what happens to your anxiety when you do this.

Date	ERP task	Anxiety ratings					
		Before task	0 mins	5 mins	15 mins	30 mins	60 mins

You have measured your anxiety over one hour. Consider what happens to it after two, three, four hours, overnight or by the next day. For your task to be useful, keep recording your anxiety until it has come down at least by half (e.g. from 6 to 3) or it is back to what it was before you did the task.

SESSION 7

CHALLENGING OCD USING ERP

OCD REVIEW

SESSION 7 PLAN

- Recap of Session 6 ☐
- Homework review ☐
- Review OCD ☐
- ERP task! ☐
- Set homework ☐
- Anything you want to add to the agenda? ☐

. . . .

. . . .

. . . .

. . . .

. . . .

RECAP: SESSION 6

In Session 6, we learned about:

- how to set up an ERP task
- how to do an ERP task.

Now let's look over your homework.

REVIEW OCD

- We know ERP is the best way to fight OCD and you have only tried it a few times, but it is good to monitor OCD.
- You may have found things have got better, worse or stayed the same since you started treatment.

 Your therapist will take a measure of your OCD in this session. Put your scores on the graph below:

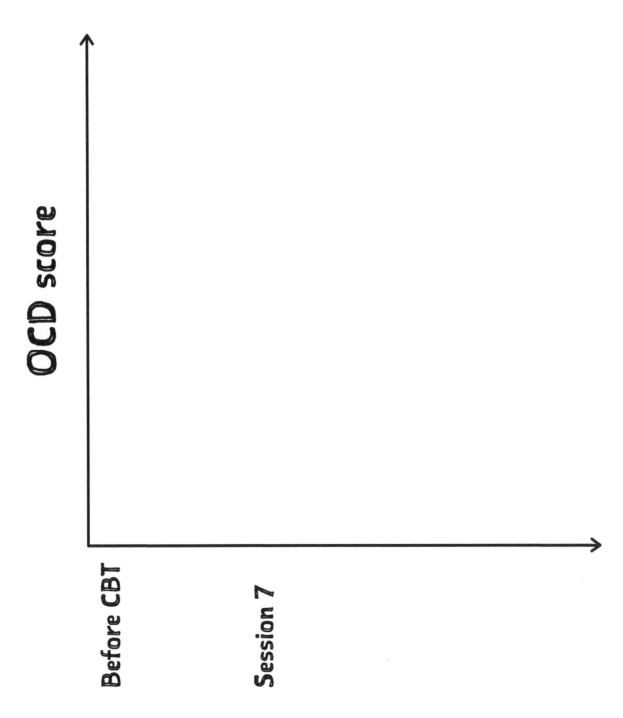

ERP TASK!

Let's do an ERP task. You will need your hierarchy from Session 5 to help us decide what to do next, or you may have had ideas after the tasks you have done so far. Don't forget your anxiety rating scale from Session 3.

STEP 1: Before we start, what level is your anxiety at the moment? Add this to the table on the next page in the column 'Before task'.

STEP 2: Pick one thing OCD makes you do or avoid or what others do from your OCD list.

. . . .

. . . .

STEP 3: What obsession does this relate to? (What is OCD telling you to worry about?)

. . . .

. . . .

STEP 4: What will the exposure be?

. . . .

. . . .

STEP 5: What will the response prevention be?

. . . .

. . . .

STEP 6: What level do you predict your anxiety will be?

. . . .

. . . .

STEP 7: Let's do the ERP task and fill out the table on the next page with your anxiety ratings. This is really important to see what happens to your anxiety over time.

STEP 8: End the task when anxiety is half of what it was at '0 mins' or it is back to the 'Before task' level.

STEP 9: What did you learn about anxiety doing this task? Did you learn anything about your obsession?

. . . .

. . . .

Well done, you completed another ERP task!

Challenge your OCD. Let's see what happens to your anxiety when you do this.

Date	ERP task!	Anxiety ratings					
		Before task	0 mins	5 mins	15 mins	30 mins	60 mins

You have measured your anxiety over one hour. Consider what happens to it after two, three, four hours, overnight or by the next day. For your task to be useful, keep recording your anxiety until it has come down at least by half (e.g. from 6 to 3) or it is back to what it was before you did the task.

HOMEWORK SESSION 7

- Read over Session 7. ☐
- Write three things you learned or remember from Session 7: ☐

. . . .

. . . .

. . . .

. . . .

- Keep adding to the hierarchy. ☐
- Practise the ERP task you did in the session (download the ERP tasks timetable to help you plan) and keep track of your progress below. Practise what you did last week and maybe some other tasks too! ☐
- Other homework: ☐

. . . .

. . . .

. . . .

. . . .

- Write down questions you or your family have for the next session: ☐

. . . .

. . . .

. . . .

. . . .

CHALLENGING OCD USING ERP

HOMEWORK: ERP TASKS!

Challenge your OCD. Let's see what happens to your anxiety when you do this.

Date	ERP task!	Anxiety ratings					
		Before task	0 mins	5 mins	15 mins	30 mins	60 mins

You have measured your anxiety over one hour. Consider what happens to it after two, three, four hours, overnight or by the next day. For your task to be useful, keep recording your anxiety until it has come down at least by half (e.g. from 6 to 3) or it is back to what it was before you did the task.

SESSION 8

CHALLENGING OCD USING ERP

SESSION 8 PLAN

- Recap of Session 7 ☐

- Homework review ☐

- ERP task! ☐

- OCD steps ☐

- Set homework ☐

- Anything you want to add to the agenda? ☐

. . . .

. . . .

. . . .

. . . .

. . . .

CHALLENGING OCD USING ERP

RECAP: SESSION 7

In Session 7, we learned about:

● what your current OCD score is

● how to continue to set up and do an ERP task.

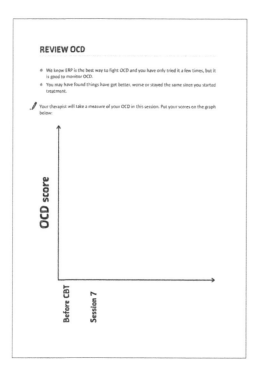

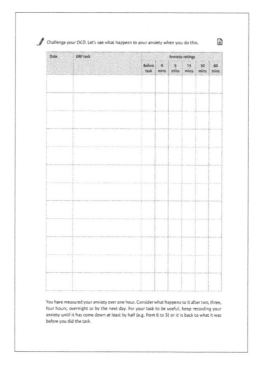

Now let's look over your homework.

ERP TASK!

Let's do an ERP task. You will need your hierarchy from Session 5 to help us decide what to do next or you may have some ideas after the tasks you have done so far. Don't forget your anxiety rating scale from Session 3.

STEP 1: Before we start, what level is your anxiety at the moment? Add this to the table on the next page in the column 'Before task'.

STEP 2: Pick one thing OCD makes you do or avoid or what others do from your OCD list.

. . . .

. . . .

STEP 3: What obsession does this relate to? (What is OCD telling you to worry about?)

. . . .

. . . .

STEP 4: What will the exposure be?

. . . .

. . . .

STEP 5: What will the response prevention be?

. . . .

. . . .

STEP 6: What level do you predict your anxiety will be?

. . . .

. . . .

STEP 7: Let's do the ERP task and fill out the table on the next page with your anxiety ratings. This is really important to see what happens to your anxiety over time.

STEP 8: End the task when anxiety is half of what it was at '0 mins' or it is back to the 'Before task' level.

STEP 9: What did you learn about anxiety doing this task? Did you learn anything about your obsession?

. . . .

. . . .

Well done, you completed another ERP task!

Challenge your OCD. Let's see what happens to your anxiety when you do this.

Date	ERP task!	Anxiety ratings					
		Before task	0 mins	5 mins	15 mins	30 mins	60 mins

You have measured your anxiety over one hour. Consider what happens to it after two, three, four hours, overnight or by the next day. For your task to be useful, keep recording your anxiety until it has come down at least by half (e.g. from 6 to 3) or it is back to what it was before you did the task.

OCD STEPS

✏️ It is helpful to break tasks down into manageable steps if it is hard to resist OCD or if the task feels too big to do. You can also choose a goal and think about steps you need to take to reach that goal. Why don't you give it a go?

Anxiety rating ☐

Anxiety rating ☐

Anxiety rating ☐

Anxiety rating ☐

Anxiety rating ☐

Anxiety rating ☐

HOMEWORK SESSION 8

● Read over Session 8. ☐

● Write three things you learned or remember from Session 8: ☐

. . . .

. . . .

. . . .

. . . .

● Keep adding to the hierarchy or OCD steps. ☐

● Practise the ERP task you did in Session 8 (download the ERP tasks timetable to help you plan) and keep track of your progress below. Practise what you did in Session 7 and maybe some other tasks too! ☐

● Other homework: ☐

. . . .

. . . .

. . . .

. . . .

● Write down questions you or your family have for the next session: ☐

. . . .

. . . .

. . . .

. . . .

CHALLENGING OCD USING ERP

91

HOMEWORK: ERP TASKS!

✎ Challenge your OCD. Let's see what happens to your anxiety when you do this.

Date	ERP task!	Anxiety ratings					
		Before task	0 mins	5 mins	15 mins	30 mins	60 mins

You have measured your anxiety over one hour. Consider what happens to it after two, three, four hours, overnight or by the next day. For your task to be useful, keep recording your anxiety until it has come down at least by half (e.g. from 6 to 3) or it is back to what it was before you did the task.

SESSION 9

SESSION 9 PLAN

- Recap of Session 8 ☐
- Homework review ☐
- ERP task! ☐
- OCD steps (optional) ☐
- Things to help you to do ERP tasks ☐
- Set homework ☐
- Anything you want to add to the agenda? ☐

....

....

....

....

....

RECAP: SESSION 8

In Session 8, we learned about:

- how to continue to set up and do an ERP task
- how to continue to use OCD steps.

Now let's look over your homework.

ERP TASK!

Let's do an ERP task. You will need your hierarchy from Session 5, or your OCD steps from Session 8, to help us decide what to do next. You may have some ideas after the tasks you have done so far. Don't forget your anxiety rating scale from Session 3.

STEP 1: Before we start, what level is your anxiety at the moment? Add this to the table on the next page in the column 'Before task'.

STEP 2: Pick one thing OCD makes you do or avoid or what others do from your OCD list or something from your OCD steps.

. . . .

. . . .

STEP 3: What obsession does this relate to? (What is OCD telling you to worry about?)

. . . .

. . . .

STEP 4: What will the exposure be?

. . . .

. . . .

STEP 5: What will the response prevention be?

. . . .

. . . .

STEP 6: What level do you predict your anxiety will be?

. . . .

. . . .

STEP 7: Let's do the ERP task and fill out the table on the next page with your anxiety ratings. This is really important to see what happens to your anxiety over time.

STEP 8: End the task when anxiety is half of what it was at '0 mins' or it is back to the 'Before task' level.

STEP 9: What did you learn about anxiety doing this task? Did you learn anything about your obsession?

. . . .

. . . .

Well done, you completed another ERP task!

Challenge your OCD. Let's see what happens to your anxiety when you do this.

Date	ERP task!	Anxiety ratings					
		Before task	0 mins	5 mins	15 mins	30 mins	60 mins

You have measured your anxiety over one hour. Consider what happens to it after two, three, four hours, overnight or by the next day. For your task to be useful, keep recording your anxiety until it has come down at least by half (e.g. from 6 to 3) or it is back to what it was before you did the task.

THINGS TO HELP YOU DO ERP

ERP tasks can sometimes be tricky and scary to do. Some people add things into their treatment to help them complete tasks, others do not need to.

If you want to try some things, here are some ideas:

Take photos or videos of when you do tasks – to remind you of all your hard work.

Keep a diary of times you have beaten OCD.

Use helpful thoughts (see the Appendix: Helpful Thoughts).

Reward yourself.

Ask your family to challenge OCD (see the Appendix:
Ask Others to Challenge OCD).

Do a survey and find out facts (see the Appendix:
Do a Survey and Find Out Facts).

Do you or your family have other ideas that may help you?

....

....

....

....

HOMEWORK SESSION 9

● Read over Session 9. ☐

● Write three things you learned or remember from Session 9. ☐

. . . .

. . . .

. . . .

. . . .

● Keep adding to the hierarchy from Session 5 or put together new step plans. ☐

● Practise the ERP task you did in Session 9 (download the ERP tasks timetable to help you plan) and keep track of your progress below. Practise tasks you have already done and maybe some other tasks too! ☐

● Try out a new thing to help you do an ERP task. ☐

● Other homework: ☐

. . . .

. . . .

. . . .

. . . .

● Write down questions you or your family have for the next session: ☐

. . . .

. . . .

. . . .

. . . .

HOMEWORK: ERP TASKS!

Challenge your OCD. Let's see what happens to your anxiety when you do this.

Date	ERP task!	Anxiety ratings					
		Before task	0 mins	5 mins	15 mins	30 mins	60 mins

You have measured your anxiety over one hour. Consider what happens to it after two, three, four hours, overnight or by the next day. For your task to be useful, keep recording your anxiety until it has come down at least by half (e.g. from 6 to 3) or it is back to what it was before you did the task.

Anxiety rating

Anxiety rating

Anxiety rating

Anxiety rating

Anxiety rating

Anxiety rating

SESSION 10

CHALLENGING OCD USING ERP

SESSION 10 PLAN

- Recap of Session 9 ☐

- Homework review ☐

- ERP task! ☐

- OCD steps (optional) ☐

- Set homework ☐

- Anything you want to add to the agenda? ☐

....

....

....

....

....

RECAP: SESSION 9

In Session 9, we learned about:

- how to continue to set up and do an ERP task
- things that can help you do ERP.

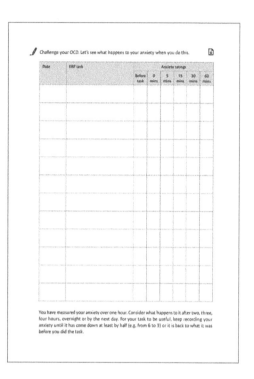

Now let's look over your homework.

ERP TASK!

Let's do an ERP task. You will need your hierarchy, or your OCD steps, to help us decide what to do next. You may have some ideas after the tasks you have done so far. Don't forget your anxiety rating scale from Session 3.

STEP 1:   Before we start, what level is your anxiety at the moment? Add this to the ERP table in the column 'Before task'.

STEP 2:   Pick one thing OCD makes you do or avoid or what others do from your OCD list or OCD steps.

. . . .

. . . .

STEP 3:   What obsession does this relate to? (What is OCD telling you to worry about?)

. . . .

. . . .

STEP 4:   What will the exposure be?

. . . .

. . . .

STEP 5:   What will the response prevention be?

. . . .

. . . .

STEP 6:   What level do you predict your anxiety will be?

. . . .

. . . .

STEP 7:   Do you need anything to help you do the ERP task?

. . . .

. . . .

STEP 8:   Let's do the ERP task and fill out the ERP table with your anxiety ratings. This is really important to see what happens to your anxiety over time.

STEP 9:   End the task when anxiety is half of what it was at '0 mins' or it is back to the 'Before task' level.

STEP 10: What did you learn about anxiety doing this task? Did you learn anything about your obsession?

. . . .

. . . .

Well done, you completed another ERP task!

Now you have done this task, what other tasks can you do that may be similar? What can you do in your day-to-day life now you have challenged OCD?

. . . .

. . . .

. . . .

. . . .

. . . .

. . . .

. . . .

107

✏️ Challenge your OCD. Let's see what happens to your anxiety when you do this. ⬇️

Date	ERP task!	Anxiety ratings					
		Before task	0 mins	5 mins	15 mins	30 mins	60 mins

You have measured your anxiety over one hour. Consider what happens to it after two, three, four hours, overnight or by the next day. For your task to be useful, keep recording your anxiety until it has come down at least by half (e.g. from 6 to 3) or it is back to what it was before you did the task.

HOMEWORK SESSION 10

- Read over Session 10.   ☐
- Write three things you learned or remember from Session 10:   ☐

. . . .

. . . .

. . . .

. . . .

- Practise the ERP task you did in Session 10 (download the ERP tasks timetable to help you plan) and keep track of your progress below. Practise what you have done in previous sessions and maybe some other tasks too!   ☐
- Other homework: ☐

. . . .

. . . .

. . . .

. . . .

- Write down questions you or your family have for the next session: ☐

. . . .

. . . .

. . . .

. . . .

CHALLENGING OCD USING ERP

HOMEWORK: ERP TASKS!

Challenge your OCD. Let's see what happens to your anxiety when you do this.

Date	ERP task!	Anxiety ratings					
		Before task	0 mins	5 mins	15 mins	30 mins	60 mins

You have measured your anxiety over one hour. Consider what happens to it after two, three, four hours, overnight or by the next day. For your task to be useful, keep recording your anxiety until it has come down at least by half (e.g. from 6 to 3) or it is back to what it was before you did the task.

HOMEWORK: ERP TASKS!

Challenge your OCD. Let's see what happens to your anxiety when you do this.

Date	ERP task!	Anxiety ratings					
		Before task	0 mins	5 mins	15 mins	30 mins	60 mins

You have measured your anxiety over one hour. Consider what happens to it after two, three, four hours, overnight or by the next day. For your task to be useful, keep recording your anxiety until it has come down at least by half (e.g. from 6 to 3) or it is back to what it was before you did the task.

SESSION 11

CHALLENGING OCD USING ERP

SESSION 11 PLAN

- Recap of Session 10 ☐
- Homework review ☐
- ERP task! ☐
- OCD steps (optional) ☐
- Set homework ☐
- Anything you want to add to the agenda? ☐

....

....

....

....

....

RECAP: SESSION 10

In Session 10, we learned about:

● how to continue to set up and do an ERP task.

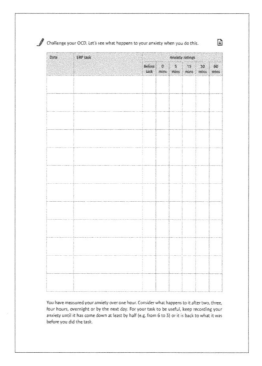

Now let's look over your homework.

ERP TASK!

Let's do an ERP task. You will need your hierarchy, or your OCD steps, to help us decide what to do next. You may have some ideas after the tasks you have done so far. Don't forget your anxiety rating scale from Session 3.

STEP 1: Before we start, what level is your anxiety at the moment? Add this to the ERP table in the column 'Before task'.

STEP 2: Pick one thing OCD makes you do or avoid or what others do from your OCD list or OCD steps.

. . . .

. . . .

STEP 3: What obsession does this relate to? (What is OCD telling you to worry about?)

. . . .

. . . .

STEP 4: What will the exposure be?

. . . .

. . . .

STEP 5: What will the response prevention be?

. . . .

. . . .

STEP 6: What level do you predict your anxiety will be?

. . . .

. . . .

STEP 7: Do you need anything to help you do the ERP task?

. . . .

. . . .

STEP 8: Let's do the ERP task and fill out the ERP table with your anxiety ratings. This is really important to see what happens to your anxiety over time.

STEP 9: End the task when anxiety is half of what it was at '0 mins' or it is back to the 'Before task' level.

STEP 10: What did you learn about anxiety doing this task? Did you learn anything about your obsession?

. . . .

. . . .

Well done, you completed another ERP task!

Now you have done this task, what other tasks can you do that may be similar? What can you do in your day-to-day life now you have challenged OCD?

. . . .

. . . .

. . . .

. . . .

. . . .

. . . .

. . . .

. . . .

✏️ Challenge your OCD. Let's see what happens to your anxiety when you do this. ⬇️

Date	ERP task!	Anxiety ratings					
		Before task	0 mins	5 mins	15 mins	30 mins	60 mins

You have measured your anxiety over one hour. Consider what happens to it after two, three, four hours, overnight or by the next day. For your task to be useful, keep recording your anxiety until it has come down at least by half (e.g. from 6 to 3) or it is back to what it was before you did the task.

HOMEWORK SESSION 11

- Read over Session 11. ☐
- Write three things you learned or remember from Session 11: ☐

  . . . .

  . . . .

  . . . .

  . . . .

- Practise the ERP task you did in Session 11 (download the ERP tasks timetable to help you plan) and keep track of your progress below. Practise what you have done in previous sessions and maybe some other tasks too! ☐
- Other homework: ☐

  . . . .

  . . . .

  . . . .

  . . . .

- Write down questions you or your family have for the next session: ☐

  . . . .

  . . . .

  . . . .

  . . . .

CHALLENGING OCD USING ERP

HOMEWORK: ERP TASKS!

Challenge your OCD. Let's see what happens to your anxiety when you do this.

Date	ERP task!	Anxiety ratings					
		Before task	0 mins	5 mins	15 mins	30 mins	60 mins

You have measured your anxiety over one hour. Consider what happens to it after two, three, four hours, overnight or by the next day. For your task to be useful, keep recording your anxiety until it has come down at least by half (e.g. from 6 to 3) or it is back to what it was before you did the task.

HOMEWORK: ERP TASKS! ⬇

✏ Challenge your OCD. Let's see what happens to your anxiety when you do this.

Date	ERP task!	Anxiety ratings					
		Before task	0 mins	5 mins	15 mins	30 mins	60 mins

You have measured your anxiety over one hour. Consider what happens to it after two, three, four hours, overnight or by the next day. For your task to be useful, keep recording your anxiety until it has come down at least by half (e.g. from 6 to 3) or it is back to what it was before you did the task.

SESSION 12

CHALLENGING
OCD USING
ERP

SESSION 12 PLAN

- Recap of Session 11 ☐
- Homework review ☐
- ERP task! ☐
- OCD steps (optional) ☐
- Rules for challenging OCD ☐
- Set homework ☐
- Anything you want to add to the agenda? ☐

. . . .

. . . .

. . . .

. . . .

. . . .

RECAP: SESSION 11

In Session 11, we learned about:

● how to continue to set up and do an ERP task.

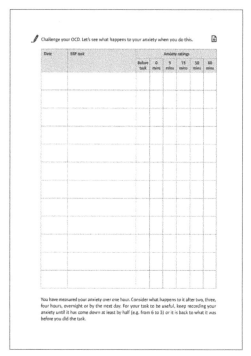

Now let's look over your homework.

ERP TASK!

Let's do an ERP task. You will need your hierarchy, or your OCD steps, to help us decide what to do next. You may have some ideas after the tasks you have done so far. Don't forget your anxiety rating scale from Session 3.

STEP 1: Before we start, what level is your anxiety at the moment? Add this to the ERP table in the column 'Before task'.

STEP 2: Pick one thing OCD makes you do or avoid or what others do from your OCD list.

. . . .

. . . .

STEP 3: What obsession does this relate to? (What is OCD telling you to worry about?)

. . . .

. . . .

STEP 4: What will the exposure be?

. . . .

. . . .

STEP 5: What will the response prevention be?

. . . .

. . . .

STEP 6: What level do you predict your anxiety will be?

. . . .

. . . .

STEP 7: Do you need anything to help you do the ERP task?

. . . .

. . . .

STEP 8: Let's do the ERP task and fill out the ERP table with your anxiety ratings. This is really important to see what happens to your anxiety over time.

STEP 9: End the task when anxiety is half of what it was at '0 mins' or it is back to the 'Before task' level.

STEP 10: What did you learn about anxiety doing this task? Did you learn anything about your obsession?

. . . .

. . . .

Well done, you completed another ERP task!

Now you have done this task, what other tasks can you do that may be similar? What can you do in your day-to-day life now you have challenged OCD?

. . . .

. . . .

. . . .

. . . .

. . . .

. . . .

. . . .

. . . .

CHALLENGING OCD USING ERP

Challenge your OCD. Let's see what happens to your anxiety when you do this.

Date	ERP task!	Anxiety ratings					
		Before task	0 mins	5 mins	15 mins	30 mins	60 mins

You have measured your anxiety over one hour. Consider what happens to it after two, three, four hours, overnight or by the next day. For your task to be useful, keep recording your anxiety until it has come down at least by half (e.g. from 6 to 3) or it is back to what it was before you did the task.

RULES FOR CHALLENGING OCD

You and your family have had lots of practice at challenging OCD.

Think together about what you think the main rules are for challenging OCD – these rules should apply no matter what OCD makes you or others do!

. . . .

. . . .

. . . .

. . . .

. . . .

. . . .

. . . .

. . . .

. . . .

. . . .

. . . .

. . . .

. . . .

. . . .

. . . .

. . . .

. . . .

. . . .

. . . . . RULES FOR CHALLENGING OCD . . . .

HOMEWORK SESSION 12

- Read over Session 12. ☐

- Practise the ERP task you did in Session 12 (download the ERP tasks timetable to help you plan) and keep track of your progress below. Practise what you have done in previous sessions and maybe some other tasks too! ☐

- Other homework: ☐

  . . . .

  . . . .

  . . . .

  . . . .

- Write three things you have learned in treatment so far: ☐

  . . . .

  . . . .

  . . . .

  . . . .

- Write down questions you or your family have for the next session: ☐

  . . . .

  . . . .

  . . . .

  . . . .

CHALLENGING OCD USING ERP

HOMEWORK: ERP TASKS!

✏ Challenge your OCD. Let's see what happens to your anxiety when you do this.

Date	ERP task!	Anxiety ratings					
		Before task	0 mins	5 mins	15 mins	30 mins	60 mins

You have measured your anxiety over one hour. Consider what happens to it after two, three, four hours, overnight or by the next day. For your task to be useful, keep recording your anxiety until it has come down at least by half (e.g. from 6 to 3) or it is back to what it was before you did the task.

HOMEWORK: ERP TASKS!

Challenge your OCD. Let's see what happens to your anxiety when you do this.

Date	ERP task!	Anxiety ratings					
		Before task	0 mins	5 mins	15 mins	30 mins	60 mins

You have measured your anxiety over one hour. Consider what happens to it after two, three, four hours, overnight or by the next day. For your task to be useful, keep recording your anxiety until it has come down at least by half (e.g. from 6 to 3) or it is back to what it was before you did the task.

SESSION 13

CHALLENGING OCD USING ERP

SESSION 13 PLAN

- Recap of Session 12 ☐
- Homework review ☐
- ERP task! ☐
- OCD steps (optional) ☐
- Set homework ☐
- Anything you want to add to the agenda? ☐

. . . .

. . . .

. . . .

. . . .

. . . .

CHALLENGING OCD USING ERP

RECAP: SESSION 12

In Session 12, we learned about:

● how to continue to set up and do an ERP task

● rules for challenging OCD.

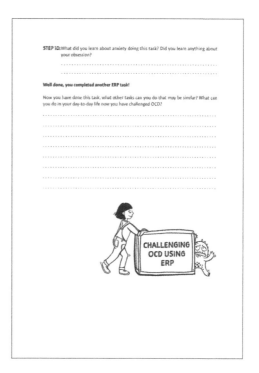

Now let's look over your homework.

ERP TASK!

Let's do an ERP task. You will need your hierarchy, or your OCD steps, to help us decide what to do next. You may have some ideas after the tasks you have done so far. Don't forget your anxiety rating scale from Session 3.

STEP 1: Before we start, what level is your anxiety at the moment? Add this to the ERP table in the column 'Before task'.

STEP 2: Pick one thing OCD makes you do or avoid or what others do from your OCD list or OCD steps.

. . . .

. . . .

STEP 3: What obsession does this relate to? (What is OCD telling you to worry about?)

. . . .

. . . .

STEP 4: What will the exposure be?

. . . .

. . . .

STEP 5: What will the response prevention be?

. . . .

. . . .

STEP 6: What level do you predict your anxiety will be?

. . . .

. . . .

STEP 7: Do you need anything to help you do the ERP task?

. . . .

. . . .

STEP 8: Let's do the ERP task and fill out the ERP table with your anxiety ratings. This is really important to see what happens to your anxiety over time.

STEP 9: End the task when anxiety is half of what it was at '0 mins' or it is back to the 'Before task' level.

STEP 10: What did you learn about anxiety doing this task? Did you learn anything about your obsession?

. . . .

. . . .

Well done, you completed another ERP task!

Now you have done this task, what other tasks can you do that may be similar? What can you do in your day-to-day life now you have challenged OCD?

. . . .

. . . .

. . . .

. . . .

. . . .

. . . .

. . . .

Challenge your OCD. Let's see what happens to your anxiety when you do this.

Date	ERP task!	Anxiety ratings					
		Before task	0 mins	5 mins	15 mins	30 mins	60 mins

You have measured your anxiety over one hour. Consider what happens to it after two, three, four hours, overnight or by the next day. For your task to be useful, keep recording your anxiety until it has come down at least by half (e.g. from 6 to 3) or it is back to what it was before you did the task.

HOMEWORK SESSION 13

- Read over Session 13. ☐
- Practise the ERP task you did in Session 13 (download the ERP tasks timetable to help you plan) and keep track of your progress below. Practise what you have done in previous sessions and maybe some other tasks too! ☐
- Other homework: ☐

. . . .

. . . .

. . . .

. . . .

- Write three things you have learned in treatment so far: ☐

. . . .

. . . .

. . . .

. . . .

- Write down questions you or your family have for the next session: ☐

. . . .

. . . .

. . . .

. . . .

CHALLENGING OCD USING ERP

HOMEWORK: ERP TASKS!

Challenge your OCD. Let's see what happens to your anxiety when you do this.

Date	ERP task!	Anxiety ratings					
		Before task	0 mins	5 mins	15 mins	30 mins	60 mins

You have measured your anxiety over one hour. Consider what happens to it after two, three, four hours, overnight or by the next day. For your task to be useful, keep recording your anxiety until it has come down at least by half (e.g. from 6 to 3) or it is back to what it was before you did the task.

HOMEWORK: ERP TASKS!

✎ Challenge your OCD. Let's see what happens to your anxiety when you do this.

Date	ERP task!	Anxiety ratings					
		Before task	0 mins	5 mins	15 mins	30 mins	60 mins

You have measured your anxiety over one hour. Consider what happens to it after two, three, four hours, overnight or by the next day. For your task to be useful, keep recording your anxiety until it has come down at least by half (e.g. from 6 to 3) or it is back to what it was before you did the task.

SESSION 14

SESSION 14 PLAN

- Recap of Session 13 ☐

- Homework review ☐

- Review OCD ☐

- ERP task! ☐

- OCD steps (optional) ☐

- Set homework ☐

- Anything you want to add to the agenda? ☐

. . . .

. . . .

. . . .

. . . .

. . . .

CHALLENGING OCD USING ERP

RECAP: SESSION 13

In Session 13, we learned about:

● how to keep challenging OCD using ERP.

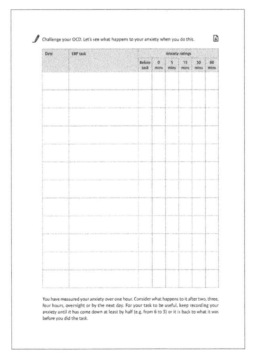

Now let's look over your homework.

REVIEW OCD

- We know that ERP is the best way to fight OCD and now you have done this lots of times.
- You may have found things have got better, worse or stayed the same since you started treatment.

 Your therapist will take a measure of your OCD in this session. Put your scores on the graph below:

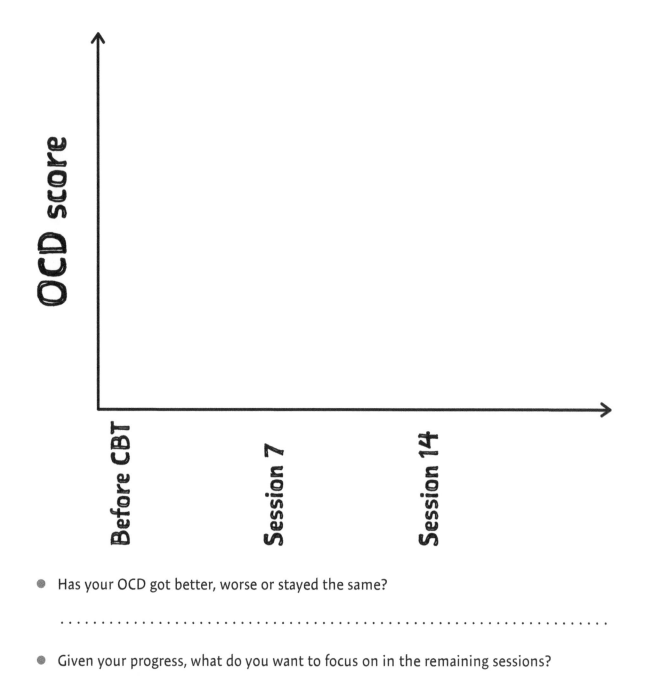

- Has your OCD got better, worse or stayed the same?

. . . .

- Given your progress, what do you want to focus on in the remaining sessions?

. . . .

. . . .

ERP TASK!

Let's do an ERP task. You will need your hierarchy, or your OCD steps, to help us decide what to do next. You may have some ideas after the tasks you have done so far. Don't forget your anxiety rating scale from Session 3.

STEP 1: Before we start, what level is your anxiety at the moment? Add this to the ERP table in the column 'Before task'.

STEP 2: Pick one thing OCD makes you do or avoid or what others do from your OCD list or OCD steps.

. . . .

. . . .

STEP 3: What obsession does this relate to? (What is OCD telling you to worry about?)

. . . .

. . . .

STEP 4: What will the exposure be?

. . . .

. . . .

STEP 5: What will the response prevention be?

. . . .

. . . .

STEP 6: What level do you predict your anxiety will be?

. . . .

. . . .

STEP 7: Do you need anything to help you do the ERP task?

. . . .

. . . .

STEP 8: Let's do the ERP task and fill out the ERP table with your anxiety ratings. This is really important to see what happens to your anxiety over time.

STEP 9: End the task when anxiety is half of what it was at '0 mins' or it is back to the 'Before task' level.

STEP 10: What did you learn about anxiety doing this task? Did you learn anything about your obsession?

. . . . 150 . . . .

. . . .

Well done, you completed another ERP task!

Now you have done this task, what other tasks can you do that may be similar? What can you do in your day-to-day life now you have challenged OCD?

. . . .

. . . .

. . . .

. . . .

. . . .

. . . .

. . . .

. . . .

Challenge your OCD. Let's see what happens to your anxiety when you do this.

Date	ERP task!	Anxiety ratings					
		Before task	0 mins	5 mins	15 mins	30 mins	60 mins

You have measured your anxiety over one hour. Consider what happens to it after two, three, four hours, overnight or by the next day. For your task to be useful, keep recording your anxiety until it has come down at least by half (e.g. from 6 to 3) or it is back to what it was before you did the task.

HOMEWORK SESSION 14

- Read over Session 14. ☐
- Practise the ERP task you did in Session 14 (download the ERP tasks timetable to help you plan) and keep track of your progress below. Practise what you have done in previous sessions and maybe some other tasks too! ☐
- Re-rate your hierarchy. ☐
- Other homework: ☐

. . . .

. . . .

. . . .

. . . .

- Write three things you have learned in treatment so far: ☐

. . . .

. . . .

. . . .

. . . .

- Write down questions you or your family have for the next session: ☐

. . . .

. . . .

. . . .

. . . .

CHALLENGING
OCD USING
ERP

HOMEWORK: ERP TASKS!

Challenge your OCD. Let's see what happens to your anxiety when you do this.

Date	ERP task!	Anxiety ratings					
		Before task	0 mins	5 mins	15 mins	30 mins	60 mins

You have measured your anxiety over one hour. Consider what happens to it after two, three, four hours, overnight or by the next day. For your task to be useful, keep recording your anxiety until it has come down at least by half (e.g. from 6 to 3) or it is back to what it was before you did the task.

HOMEWORK: ERP TASKS! ⤓

✏ Challenge your OCD. Let's see what happens to your anxiety when you do this.

Date	ERP task!	Anxiety ratings					
		Before task	0 mins	5 mins	15 mins	30 mins	60 mins

You have measured your anxiety over one hour. Consider what happens to it after two, three, four hours, overnight or by the next day. For your task to be useful, keep recording your anxiety until it has come down at least by half (e.g. from 6 to 3) or it is back to what it was before you did the task.

HOMEWORK: RE-RATE YOUR HIERARCHY

In Session 5, we put all the things OCD makes you and others do or avoid in order, starting with what would make you less anxious to challenge, up to what would be the hardest thing to do.

Now you have done lots of ERP tasks, let's see what OCD symptoms are left and put them in order.

Compulsion/Avoid/What others do	Anxiety rating

Compulsion/Avoid/What others do	Anxiety rating
157	
Compulsion/Avoid/What others do	Anxiety rating

Compulsion/Avoid/What others do	Anxiety rating
158	
Compulsion/Avoid/What others do	Anxiety rating

Compulsion/Avoid/What others do	Anxiety rating
159	
Compulsion/Avoid/What others do	Anxiety rating

SESSION 15

CHALLENGING
OCD USING ERP
— YOU TAKE
CHARGE

SESSION 15 PLAN

- Recap of Session 14 ☐

- Homework review ☐

- ERP task! ☐

- OCD steps (optional) ☐

- Things to help you do ERP ☐

- Set homework ☐

- Anything you want to add to the agenda? ☐

. . . .

. . . .

. . . .

. . . .

. . . .

RECAP: SESSION 14

In Session 14, we learned about:

- how to continue to set up and do an ERP task
- what OCD symptoms are left to tackle.

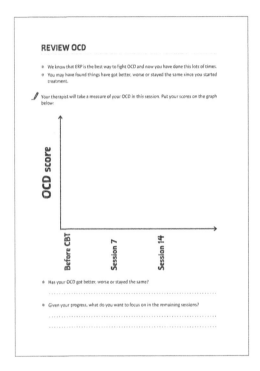

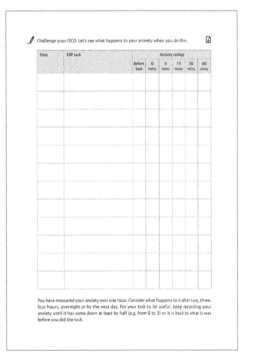

Now let's look over your homework.

ERP TASK!

Let's do an ERP task. You will need the hierarchy that you updated for your homework in the last session, or your OCD steps, to help us decide what to do next. You may have some ideas after the tasks you have done so far. Don't forget your anxiety rating scale from Session 3. This time, you and your family can decide and plan the task together.

STEP 1: Before we start, what level is your anxiety at the moment? Add this to the ERP table in the column 'Before task'.

STEP 2: Pick one thing OCD makes you do or avoid or what others do from your OCD list or OCD steps.

. . . .

. . . .

STEP 3: What obsession does this relate to? (What is OCD telling you to worry about?)

. . . .

. . . .

STEP 4: What will the exposure be?

. . . .

. . . .

STEP 5: What will the response prevention be?

. . . .

. . . .

STEP 6: What level do you predict your anxiety will be?

. . . .

. . . .

STEP 7: Do you need anything to help you do the ERP task?

. . . .

. . . .

STEP 8: Let's do the ERP task and fill out the ERP table with your anxiety ratings. This is really important to see what happens to your anxiety over time.

STEP 9: End the task when anxiety is half of what it was at '0 mins' or it is back to the 'Before task' level.

STEP 10: What did you learn about anxiety doing this task? Did you learn anything about your obsession?

. . . . 165 . . . .

. . . .

Well done, you completed another ERP task!

Now you have done this task, what other tasks can you do that may be similar? What can you do in your day-to-day life now you have challenged OCD?

. . . .

. . . .

. . . .

. . . .

. . . .

. . . .

. . . .

. . . .

✏ Challenge your OCD. Let's see what happens to your anxiety when you do this. ⬇

Date	ERP task!	Anxiety ratings					
		Before task	0 mins	5 mins	15 mins	30 mins	60 mins

You have measured your anxiety over one hour. Consider what happens to it after two, three, four hours, overnight or by the next day. For your task to be useful, keep recording your anxiety until it has come down at least by half (e.g. from 6 to 3) or it is back to what it was before you did the task.

THINGS TO HELP YOU DO ERP

Do you remember the things that you could add to ERP tasks to help you do them?

Let's have a look and see if there are some you want to try now.

Take photos or videos of when you do tasks – to remind you of all your hard work.

Keep a diary of times you have beaten OCD.

Use helpful thoughts (see the Appendix: Helpful Thoughts).

Reward yourself.

Ask your family to challenge OCD (see the Appendix:
Ask Others to Challenge OCD).

Do a survey and find out facts (see the Appendix:
Do a Survey and Find Out Facts).

Do you or your family have other ideas that may help you?

. . . .

. . . .

. . . .

. . . .

HOMEWORK SESSION 15

- Read over Session 15. ☐
- Practise the ERP task you did in Session 15 (download the ERP tasks timetable to help you plan) and keep track of your progress below. Practise what you have done in previous sessions and maybe some other tasks too! ☐
- Other homework: ☐

. . . .

. . . .

. . . .

. . . .

- Write three things you have learned in treatment so far: ☐

. . . .

. . . .

. . . .

. . . .

- Write down questions you or your family have for the next session: ☐

. . . .

. . . .

. . . .

. . . .

CHALLENGING OCD USING ERP – YOU TAKE CHARGE

HOMEWORK: ERP TASKS!

✏️ Challenge your OCD. Let's see what happens to your anxiety when you do this.

Date	ERP task!	Anxiety ratings					
		Before task	0 mins	5 mins	15 mins	30 mins	60 mins

You have measured your anxiety over one hour. Consider what happens to it after two, three, four hours, overnight or by the next day. For your task to be useful, keep recording your anxiety until it has come down at least by half (e.g. from 6 to 3) or it is back to what it was before you did the task.

HOMEWORK: ERP TASKS! ⬇

✏️ Challenge your OCD. Let's see what happens to your anxiety when you do this.

Date	ERP task!	Anxiety ratings					
		Before task	0 mins	5 mins	15 mins	30 mins	60 mins

You have measured your anxiety over one hour. Consider what happens to it after two, three, four hours, overnight or by the next day. For your task to be useful, keep recording your anxiety until it has come down at least by half (e.g. from 6 to 3) or it is back to what it was before you did the task.

SESSION 16

CHALLENGING
OCD USING ERP
– YOU TAKE
CHARGE

SESSION 16 PLAN

- Recap of Session 15 ☐
- Homework review ☐
- ERP task! ☐
- OCD steps (optional) ☐
- Set homework ☐
- Anything you want to add to the agenda? ☐

. . . .

. . . .

. . . .

. . . .

. . . .

CHALLENGING OCD USING ERP – YOU TAKE CHARGE

RECAP: SESSION 15

In Session 15, we learned about:

● how to continue to set up and do an ERP task

● things to help you do ERP tasks.

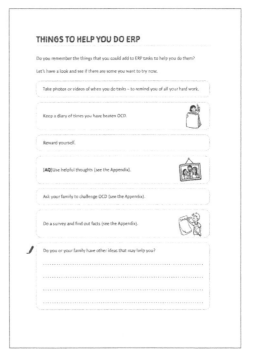

Now let's look over your homework.

ERP TASK!

Let's do an ERP task. You will need your updated hierarchy or your OCD steps, to help us decide what to do next. You may have some ideas after the tasks you have done so far. Don't forget your anxiety rating scale from Session 3. This time, you and your family can decide and plan the task together.

STEP 1: Before we start, what level is your anxiety at the moment? Add this to the ERP table in the column 'Before task'.

STEP 2: Pick one thing OCD makes you do or avoid or what others do from your OCD list or OCD steps.

. . . .

. . . .

STEP 3: What obsession does this relate to? (What is OCD telling you to worry about?)

. . . .

. . . .

STEP 4: What will the exposure be?

. . . .

. . . .

STEP 5: What will the response prevention be?

. . . .

. . . .

STEP 6: What level do you predict your anxiety will be?

. . . .

. . . .

STEP 7: Do you need anything to help you do the ERP task?

. . . .

. . . .

STEP 8: Let's do the ERP task and fill out the ERP table with your anxiety ratings. This is really important to see what happens to your anxiety over time.

STEP 9: End the task when anxiety is half of what it was at '0 mins' or it is back to the 'Before task' level.

STEP 10: What did you learn about anxiety doing this task? Did you learn anything about your obsession?

. . . .

. . . .

Well done, you completed another ERP task!

Now you have done this task, what other tasks can you do that may be similar? What can you do in your day-to-day life now you have challenged OCD?

. . . .

. . . .

. . . .

. . . .

. . . .

. . . .

. . . .

. . . .

Challenge your OCD. Let's see what happens to your anxiety when you do this.

Date	ERP task!	Anxiety ratings					
		Before task	0 mins	5 mins	15 mins	30 mins	60 mins

You have measured your anxiety over one hour. Consider what happens to it after two, three, four hours, overnight or by the next day. For your task to be useful, keep recording your anxiety until it has come down at least by half (e.g. from 6 to 3) or it is back to what it was before you did the task.

HOMEWORK SESSION 16

- Read over Session 16. ☐

- Practise the ERP task you did in Session 16 (download the ERP tasks timetable to help you plan) and keep track of your progress below. Practise what you have done in previous sessions and maybe some other tasks too! ☐

- Other homework: ☐

....

....

....

....

- Write three things you have learned from treatment so far: ☐

....

....

....

....

- Write down questions you or your family have for the next session: ☐

....

....

....

....

CHALLENGING OCD USING ERP – YOU TAKE CHARGE

HOMEWORK: ERP TASKS!

Challenge your OCD. Let's see what happens to your anxiety when you do this.

Date	ERP task!	Anxiety ratings					
		Before task	0 mins	5 mins	15 mins	30 mins	60 mins

You have measured your anxiety over one hour. Consider what happens to it after two, three, four hours, overnight or by the next day. For your task to be useful, keep recording your anxiety until it has come down at least by half (e.g. from 6 to 3) or it is back to what it was before you did the task.

HOMEWORK: ERP TASKS!

Challenge your OCD. Let's see what happens to your anxiety when you do this.

Date	ERP task!	Anxiety ratings					
		Before task	0 mins	5 mins	15 mins	30 mins	60 mins

You have measured your anxiety over one hour. Consider what happens to it after two, three, four hours, overnight or by the next day. For your task to be useful, keep recording your anxiety until it has come down at least by half (e.g. from 6 to 3) or it is back to what it was before you did the task.

SESSION 17

SESSION 17 PLAN

- Recap of Session 16 ☐

- Homework review ☐

- ERP task! ☐

- OCD steps (optional) ☐

- Set homework ☐

- Anything you want to add to the agenda? ☐

....

....

....

....

....

RECAP: SESSION 16

In Session 16, we learned about:

● how to continue to set up and do an ERP task.

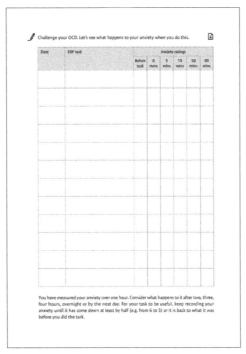

Now let's look over your homework.

ERP TASK!

Let's do an ERP task. You will need your updated hierarchy, or your OCD steps, to help us decide what to do next. You may have some ideas after the tasks you have done so far. Don't forget your anxiety rating scale from Session 3. This time, you and your family can decide and plan the task together.

STEP 1: Before we start, what level is your anxiety at the moment? Add this to the ERP table in the column 'Before task'.

STEP 2: Pick one thing OCD makes you do or avoid or what others do from your OCD list or OCD steps.

. . . .

. . . .

STEP 3: What obsession does this relate to? (What is OCD telling you to worry about?)

. . . .

. . . .

STEP 4: What will the exposure be?

. . . .

. . . .

STEP 5: What will the response prevention be?

. . . .

. . . .

STEP 6: What level do you predict your anxiety will be?

. . . .

. . . .

STEP 7: Do you need anything to help you do the ERP task?

. . . .

. . . .

STEP 8: Let's do the ERP task and fill out the ERP table with your anxiety ratings. This is really important to see what happens to your anxiety over time.

STEP 9: End the task when anxiety is half of what it was at '0 mins' or it is back to the 'Before task' level.

STEP 10: What did you learn about anxiety doing this task? Did you learn anything about your obsession?

. . . .

. . . .

Well done, you completed another ERP task!

Now you have done this task, what other tasks can you do that may be similar? What can you do in your day-to-day life now you have challenged OCD?

. . . .

. . . .

. . . .

. . . .

. . . .

. . . .

. . . .

. . . .

Challenge your OCD. Let's see what happens to your anxiety when you do this.

Date	ERP task!	Anxiety ratings					
		Before task	0 mins	5 mins	15 mins	30 mins	60 mins

You have measured your anxiety over one hour. Consider what happens to it after two, three, four hours, overnight or by the next day. For your task to be useful, keep recording your anxiety until it has come down at least by half (e.g. from 6 to 3) or it is back to what it was before you did the task.

HOMEWORK SESSION 17

- Read over Session 17. ☐
- Practise the ERP task you did in Session 17 (download the ERP tasks timetable to help you plan) and keep track of your progress below. Practise what you have done in previous sessions and maybe some other tasks too! ☐
- Other homework: ☐

. . . .

. . . .

. . . .

. . . .

- Write three things you have learned in treatment so far: ☐

. . . .

. . . .

. . . .

. . . .

- Write down questions you or your family have for the next session: ☐

. . . .

. . . .

. . . .

. . . .

CHALLENGING OCD USING ERP – YOU TAKE CHARGE

HOMEWORK: ERP TASKS!

Challenge your OCD. Let's see what happens to your anxiety when you do this.

Date	ERP task!	Anxiety ratings					
		Before task	0 mins	5 mins	15 mins	30 mins	60 mins

You have measured your anxiety over one hour. Consider what happens to it after two, three, four hours, overnight or by the next day. For your task to be useful, keep recording your anxiety until it has come down at least by half (e.g. from 6 to 3) or it is back to what it was before you did the task.

HOMEWORK: ERP TASKS!

✐ Challenge your OCD. Let's see what happens to your anxiety when you do this.

Date	ERP task!	Anxiety ratings					
		Before task	0 mins	5 mins	15 mins	30 mins	60 mins

You have measured your anxiety over one hour. Consider what happens to it after two, three, four hours, overnight or by the next day. For your task to be useful, keep recording your anxiety until it has come down at least by half (e.g. from 6 to 3) or it is back to what it was before you did the task.

SESSION 18

SESSION 18 PLAN

- Recap of Session 17 ☐
- Homework review ☐
- ERP task! ☐
- OCD steps (optional) ☐
- Set homework ☐
- Anything you want to add to the agenda? ☐

. . . .

. . . .

. . . .

. . . .

. . . .

CHALLENGING OCD USING ERP – YOU TAKE CHARGE

RECAP: SESSION 17

In Session 17, we learned about:

● how to continue to set up and do an ERP task.

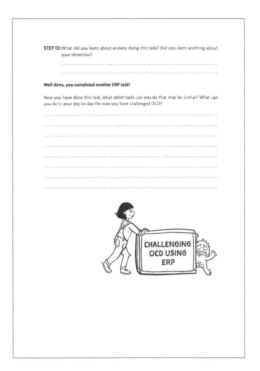

Now let's look over your homework.

ERP TASK!

Let's do an ERP task. You will need your updated hierarchy, or your OCD steps, to help us decide what to do next. You may have some ideas after the tasks you have done so far. Don't forget your anxiety rating scale from Session 3. This time, you and your family can decide and plan the task together.

STEP 1: Before we start, what level is your anxiety at the moment? Add this to the ERP table in the column 'Before task'.

STEP 2: Pick one thing OCD makes you do or avoid or what others do from your OCD list.

. . . .

. . . .

STEP 3: What obsession does this relate to? (What is OCD telling you to worry about?)

. . . .

. . . .

STEP 4: What will the exposure be?

. . . .

. . . .

STEP 5: What will the response prevention be?

. . . .

. . . .

STEP 6: What level do you predict your anxiety will be?

. . . .

. . . .

STEP 7: Do you need anything to help you do the ERP task?

. . . .

. . . .

STEP 8: Let's do the ERP task and fill out the ERP table with your anxiety ratings. This is really important to see what happens to your anxiety over time.

STEP 9: End the task when anxiety is half of what it was at '0 mins' or it is back to the 'Before task' level.

STEP 10: What did you learn about anxiety doing this task? Did you learn anything about your obsession?

. . . .

. . . .

Well done, you completed another ERP task!

Now you have done this task, what other tasks can you do that may be similar? What can you do in your day-to-day life now you have challenged OCD?

. . . .

. . . .

. . . .

. . . .

. . . .

. . . .

. . . .

. . . .

CHALLENGING OCD USING ERP

197

Challenge your OCD. Let's see what happens to your anxiety when you do this.

Date	ERP task!	Anxiety ratings					
		Before task	0 mins	5 mins	15 mins	30 mins	60 mins

You have measured your anxiety over one hour. Consider what happens to it after two, three, four hours, overnight or by the next day. For your task to be useful, keep recording your anxiety until it has come down at least by half (e.g. from 6 to 3) or it is back to what it was before you did the task.

Anxiety rating

Anxiety rating

Anxiety rating

Anxiety rating

Anxiety rating

Anxiety rating

HOMEWORK SESSION 18

- Read over Session 18. ☐

- Practise the ERP task you did in Session 18 (download the ERP tasks timetable to help you plan) and keep track of your progress below. Practise what you have done in previous sessions and maybe some other tasks too! ☐

- Other homework: ☐

....

....

....

....

- Write three things you have learned in treatment so far: ☐

....

....

....

....

- Write down questions you or your family have for the next session: ☐

....

....

....

....

HOMEWORK: ERP TASKS!

Challenge your OCD. Let's see what happens to your anxiety when you do this.

Date	ERP task!	Anxiety ratings					
		Before task	0 mins	5 mins	15 mins	30 mins	60 mins

You have measured your anxiety over one hour. Consider what happens to it after two, three, four hours, overnight or by the next day. For your task to be useful, keep recording your anxiety until it has come down at least by half (e.g. from 6 to 3) or it is back to what it was before you did the task.

HOMEWORK: ERP TASKS!

✏ Challenge your OCD. Let's see what happens to your anxiety when you do this.

Date	ERP task!	Anxiety ratings					
		Before task	0 mins	5 mins	15 mins	30 mins	60 mins

You have measured your anxiety over one hour. Consider what happens to it after two, three, four hours, overnight or by the next day. For your task to be useful, keep recording your anxiety until it has come down at least by half (e.g. from 6 to 3) or it is back to what it was before you did the task.

SESSION 19

CHALLENGING OCD USING ERP AND GETTING READY FOR THE FINISH

SESSION 19 PLAN

- Recap of Session 18 ☐
- Homework review ☐
- ERP or extreme task! ☐
- OCD steps (optional) ☐
- Getting ready for the finish ☐
- Set homework ☐
- Anything you want to add to the agenda? ☐

....
....
....
....
....

CHALLENGING OCD USING ERP AND GETTING READY FOR THE FINISH

RECAP: SESSION 18

In Session 18, we learned about:

● how to continue to set up and do an ERP task.

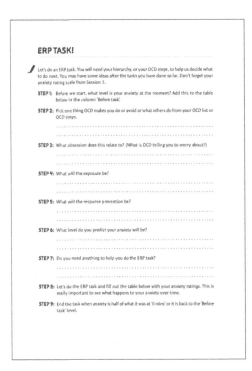

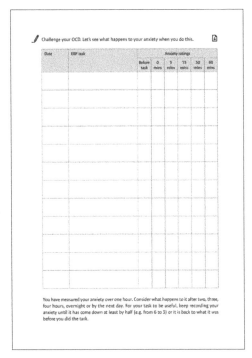

Now let's look over your homework.

ERP OR EXTREME TASK!

Let's do an ERP task. Sometimes at this stage in treatment people like to do an extreme task to really show OCD you are the boss (see the Appendix: Extreme Tasks). It is up to you! You will need your updated hierarchy from Session 14, or your OCD steps, to help us decide what to do next. You may have some ideas after the tasks you have done so far. Don't forget your anxiety rating scale from Session 3. This time, you and your family can decide and plan the task together.

STEP 1: Before we start, what level is your anxiety at the moment? Add this to the ERP table in the column 'Before task'.

STEP 2: Pick one thing OCD makes you do or avoid or what others do from your OCD list.

. . . .

. . . .

STEP 3: What obsession does this relate to? (What is OCD telling you to worry about?)

. . . .

. . . .

STEP 4: What will the exposure be?

. . . .

. . . .

STEP 5: What will the response prevention be?

. . . .

. . . .

STEP 6: What level do you predict your anxiety will be?

. . . .

. . . .

STEP 7: Do you need anything to help you do the ERP task?

. . . .

. . . .

STEP 8: Let's do the ERP task and fill out the ERP table with your anxiety ratings. This is really important to see what happens to your anxiety over time.

STEP 9: End the task when anxiety is half of what it was at '0 mins' or it is back to the 'Before task' level.

STEP 10: What did you learn about anxiety doing this task? Did you learn anything about your obsession?

. . . .

. . . .

Well done, you completed another ERP task!

Now you have done this task, what other tasks can you do that may be similar? What can you do in your day-to-day life now you have challenged OCD?

. . . .

. . . .

. . . .

. . . .

. . . .

. . . .

. . . .

. . . .

Challenge your OCD. Let's see what happens to your anxiety when you do this.

Date	ERP task!	Anxiety ratings					
		Before task	0 mins	5 mins	15 mins	30 mins	60 mins

You have measured your anxiety over one hour. Consider what happens to it after two, three, four hours, overnight or by the next day. For your task to be useful, keep recording your anxiety until it has come down at least by half (e.g. from 6 to 3) or it is back to what it was before you did the task.

GETTING READY FOR THE FINISH

You don't have long until your regular CBT for OCD sessions are coming to an end. It is time to get ready to continue challenging OCD without the support of your therapist. Let's get ready for the finish.

- What OCD symptoms have you been able to challenge in CBT? Have a look through your workbook to remind yourself.

. . . .

. . . .

- How did you challenge these symptoms?

. . . .

. . . .

- Do you have any OCD symptoms left to work on? If so, let's make a list.

. . . .

. . . .

- What is your plan to challenge these symptoms? Look at your rules for challenging OCD to help you.

. . . .

. . . .

Anxiety rating

Anxiety rating

Anxiety rating

Anxiety rating

Anxiety rating

Anxiety rating

HOMEWORK SESSION 19

- Read over Session 19. ☐

- Practise the ERP task you did in Session 19 (download the ERP tasks timetable to help you plan) and keep track of your progress below. Practise what you have done in previous sessions and maybe some other tasks too! ☐

- Read Session 20 to prepare for the next session. ☐

- Other homework: ☐

. . . .

. . . .

. . . .

. . . .

- Write three things you have learned in treatment so far: ☐

. . . .

. . . .

. . . .

. . . .

- Write down questions you or your family have for the next session: ☐

. . . .

. . . .

. . . .

. . . .

CHALLENGING OCD USING ERP AND GETTING READY FOR THE FINISH

HOMEWORK: ERP TASKS!

Challenge your OCD. Let's see what happens to your anxiety when you do this.

Date	ERP task!	Anxiety ratings					
		Before task	0 mins	5 mins	15 mins	30 mins	60 mins

You have measured your anxiety over one hour. Consider what happens to it after two, three, four hours, overnight or by the next day. For your task to be useful, keep recording your anxiety until it has come down at least by half (e.g. from 6 to 3) or it is back to what it was before you did the task.

HOMEWORK: ERP TASKS!

Challenge your OCD. Let's see what happens to your anxiety when you do this.

Date	ERP task!	Anxiety ratings					
		Before task	0 mins	5 mins	15 mins	30 mins	60 mins

You have measured your anxiety over one hour. Consider what happens to it after two, three, four hours, overnight or by the next day. For your task to be useful, keep recording your anxiety until it has come down at least by half (e.g. from 6 to 3) or it is back to what it was before you did the task.

SESSION 20

RELAPSE PREVENTION PLAN

SESSION 20 PLAN

- Recap of Session 19
- Homework review
- Relapse prevention plan
- Review OCD
- OCD steps (optional)
- Planning ahead
- Anything you want to add to the agenda?

. . . .

. . . .

. . . .

. . . .

. . . .

RELAPSE PREVENTION PLAN

RECAP: SESSION 19

In Session 19, we learned about:

● how to continue to set up and do an ERP task.

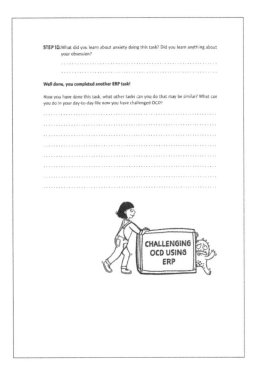
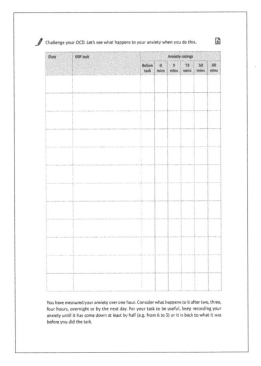

Now let's look over your homework.

RELAPSE PREVENTION PLAN

- You have worked hard in treatment and you have learned how to challenge OCD.
- Let's have a look at your goals from Session 5 and see what you have achieved and the things you are still working on.
- You and your family have to keep working hard to keep OCD away and to challenge the remaining symptoms.
- You have had lots of practice challenging OCD, so you know what to do.

Let's write a plan you can look at after the sessions have ended.

What do you think might trigger OCD coming back? Do you have anything stressful coming up?

....

....

....

What sort of OCD symptoms might be the most likely to sneak back? What will be the warning signs of it coming back?

....

....

....

What would you or someone else notice?

....

....

....

Who would you tell if you notice OCD coming back?

....

....

....

What should you do if the symptoms come back? (Look at your rules from Session 12 to help you.)

....

....

....

Remember to tell someone as soon as you notice OCD coming back, and act early!

What activities can you do now that OCD isn't taking up so much time? It is important to keep doing these activities as OCD might try to sneak back if you're bored!

....

....

....

REVIEW OCD

- We know ERP is the best way to fight OCD and you have now done this lots of times.
- You may have found that things have got better, worse or stayed the same since you started treatment.

Your therapist will take a measure of your OCD in this session. Put your scores on the graph below:

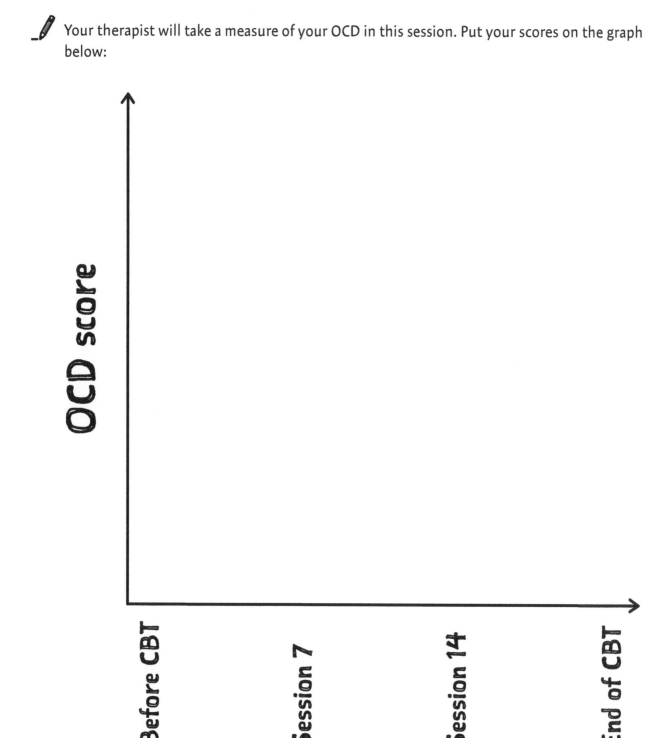

PLANNING AHEAD

✏️ Let's have a think about what you need to work on between now and your next follow-up.

Write a list of what you need to do before then:

. . . .

. . . .

. . . .

Do you need an OCD steps plan or timetable?

. . . .

. . . .

. . . .

What are you looking forward to doing now that you couldn't do before because of OCD?

. . . .

. . . .

. . . .

Do you want to add any new goals to your list from Session 5?

. . . .

. . . .

. . . .

Certificate

WELL DONE!

You have worked hard
to challenge OCD!

APPENDIX

THINGS TO HELP YOU IN TREATMENT

DIFFERENT FEELINGS

Some people find it difficult to recognize different feelings or to tell the difference between them.

Let's look at each of the different feelings below. Tick and make a list of what you would notice if you felt that way.

Smiling or laughing ☐

Calm ☐

Muscles relaxed ☐

. . . .

. . . .

Happy

Crying ☐

Body feels heavy ☐

No energy ☐

. . . .

. . . .

Sad

Feel tense ☐

Clenched fists ☐

Feeling hot ☐

. . . .

. . . .

Angry

What other feelings can you think of?

. . . .

. . . .

. . . .

. . . .

. . . .

LEARNING ABOUT THOUGHTS

- We all get lots of different types of thoughts – we spoke about some of the ones in OCD and ASD earlier.

- Did you know that everyone (including people without OCD) gets thoughts that pop into their heads that they do not want to have – they are called intrusive thoughts. They come in like an intruder.

- These thoughts can be scary, strange, horrible or rude.

- There have been surveys done on hundreds of people that found people with and without OCD have the same intrusive thoughts. The difference is, people without OCD can just ignore them and think 'that's just a thought'.

- Ask your family or your therapist – do they get thoughts that pop into their heads that they do not like? What kind of thoughts do they get?

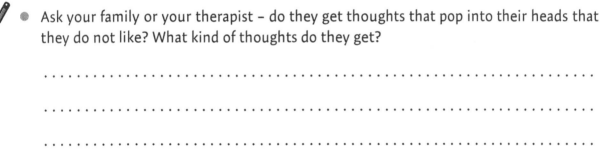

- Thoughts aren't facts – our brains come up with lots of thoughts all the time and most are random.

- We cannot control all our thoughts and we do not need lots of the thoughts we get.

LEARNING ABOUT THOUGHTS

OCD can sometimes trick us into thinking our thoughts are powerful or can make things come true.

Let's try this out:

- Think of something you would really like to happen, such as finding £10 under your chair. Think really hard about it...did it come true?

- Now think of something bad happening, such as your therapist walking around the room and falling over or the cars outside crashing. Did it happen?

What does this tell you about the power of thoughts?

....

....

....

....

....

....

....

....

....

....

....

HELPFUL THOUGHTS

- OCD can put lots of annoying thoughts in your head.

- It can be helpful to have some things you can say back to OCD in your head to help you do ERP tasks.

- Have a look below and try some of these out to see if it helps you.

Add some helpful thoughts you can use to boss back OCD.

Be careful that these do not become a way to reassure yourself, as this is a compulsion!

ASK OTHERS TO CHALLENGE OCD

- We have been talking about what families and others have to do for OCD – this is what we call (family) accommodation.
- Every family is affected by OCD and often OCD bosses them around too. This can include:
  - giving reassurance
  - helping with compulsions
  - avoiding things that OCD does not like
  - changing plans and routines because of OCD.

  You will have other examples on your OCD hierarchy.
- To challenge OCD, make sure everything others are doing for OCD is on your list and that they are challenged step by step using ERP in the same way as other compulsions.
- It is important that you all agree together when this is to be challenged and what the plan is using the ERP task sheets.
- It is important that if more than one person is doing things for OCD, such as teachers and friends, they challenge the same OCD symptoms, at the same time and in exactly the same way. OCD is very sneaky and will try to get someone to give in to it! Use the ERP task timetable sheets to help you plan this.

REASSURANCE SEEKING

- This is a common way OCD gets other people involved – it makes you ask questions or get others to say things to reduce anxiety (like every other compulsion).

- So, the way to challenge it is to use...ERP!

- OCD can ask for reassurance in very sneaky ways, so let's have a think together about how OCD gets reassurance from others:

....

....

....

....

....

WAYS TO RESPOND TO OCD REASSURANCE SEEKING

Now we have listed the ways OCD gets reassurance, let's think together about alternative things people can do or say to challenge OCD. Here are some options:

- Ignore the OCD question and change the subject.

- Reply and say 'that sounds like an OCD question, I can't answer that' or 'let's challenge OCD and ignore it'.

- Can you think of other options?

....

....

....

....

....

Remember, it is important when challenging OCD that everyone who gets asked for reassurance responds in the same way.

DO A SURVEY OR FIND OUT FACTS

- OCD can make us forget what is 'normal' or typical to do. It can make people behave in unusual ways, and sometimes you may have been doing it for so long, you and other people have got used to it!

- OCD can also make us very confused about what is fact and what is fiction. It can play tricks on us, saying things are dangerous when they are not, or that the risk of something bad happening is higher than it is. It can trick us in lots of different ways!

- A good way to challenge OCD is to do a survey or some research to get some facts.

- It is important when you find out facts or complete a survey, that you do this once and do not keep doing it or telling yourself facts over and over, as that can become a compulsion. You will know it is a compulsion if you feel you have to do it to bring your anxiety down.

Let's plan a survey or topics to research.

What will you ask or search for?

. . . .

. . . .

. . . .

. . . .

. . . .

. . . .

. . . .

Who will you ask or where will you search?

. . . .

. . . .

. . . .

. . . .

. . . .

. . . .

. . . .

What were the results of your survey?

. . . .

. . . .

. . . .

. . . .

. . . .

. . . .

. . . .

What have you learned from the survey?

. . . .

. . . .

. . . .

. . . .

. . . .

. . . .

. . . .

EXTREME TASKS

- These tasks are good to do after you have tackled most of your compulsions – even when you have reached the top of your hierarchy or OCD steps plan.

- This involves going beyond the top of your hierarchy so you can push OCD to the limit and prove it cannot control you. These are called overlearning tasks.

- Overlearning tasks are not things you have to do day to day like your other ERP tasks but are one-off tasks to show OCD you have beaten it!

- Your therapist will give you some ideas of overlearning tasks.

- Think together with your therapist what your overlearning tasks could be. What is the obsession you are challenging and how could this task help you in conquering that once and for all?

. . . .

. . . .

. . . .

. . . .

. . . .

. . . .

. . . .

. . . .

. . . .

. . . .

. . . .

. . . .

. . . .

FOLLOW-UP 1

FOLLOW-UP 1 PLAN

- Review and plan ☐

- Review and measure OCD ☐

- Anything you want to add to the agenda? ☐

....

....

....

....

....

....

....

REVIEW AND PLAN

Let's have a look over what we did last session:

- Did you manage to stick to the plan we came up with? What went well and what was tricky?

  . . . .

  . . . .

- What OCD symptoms have you kept away?

  . . . .

  . . . .

- What parts of OCD have been tricky to manage?

  . . . .

  . . . .

- Let's have a look at your relapse prevention plan from Session 20. Is there anything we need to change on it?

  . . . .

  . . . .

- Let's come up with a plan on how to tackle parts of OCD that are still troubling you. What do you need?

- Is there anything coming up that may make it difficult to do the plan? What can you do to overcome this?

  . . . .

  . . . .

REVIEW AND MEASURE OCD (OPTIONAL)

- You may have found that things have got better, worse or stayed the same since your last session.
- Your therapist will take a measure of your OCD in this session. Put your scores on the graph below:

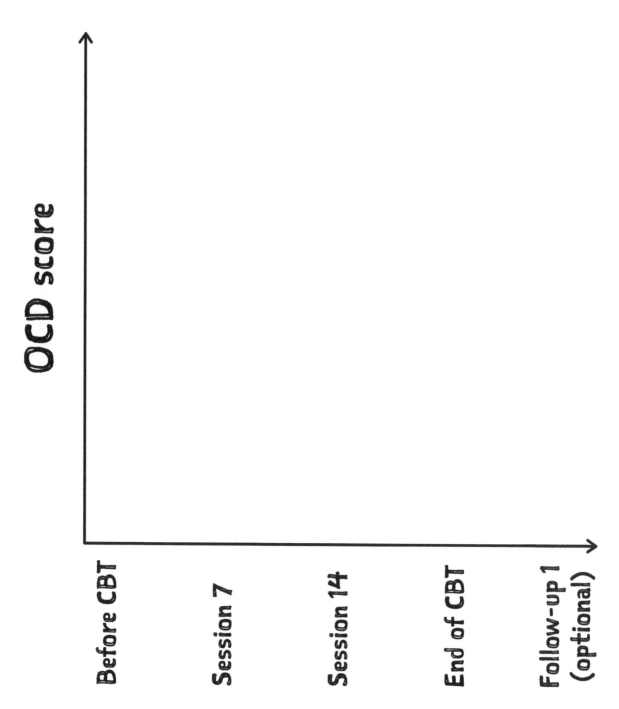

FOLLOW-UP 2

FOLLOW-UP 2 PLAN

- Review and plan ☐

- Review and measure OCD ☐

- Anything you want to add to the agenda? ☐

....

....

....

....

....

....

....

REVIEW AND PLAN

Let's have a look over what we did last session:

- Did you manage to stick to the plan we came up with? What went well and what was tricky?

  ....

  ....

- What OCD symptoms have you kept away?

  ....

  ....

- What parts of OCD have been tricky to manage?

  ....

  ....

- Let's have a look at your relapse prevention plan from Session 20. Is there anything we need to change on it?

  ....

  ....

- Let's come up with a plan on how to tackle parts of OCD that are still troubling you. What do you need?

- Is there anything coming up that may make it difficult to do the plan? What can you do to overcome this?

  ....

  ....

REVIEW AND MEASURE OCD

- You may have found that things have got better, worse or stayed the same since your last session.

- Your therapist will take a measure of your OCD in this session. Put your scores on the graph below:

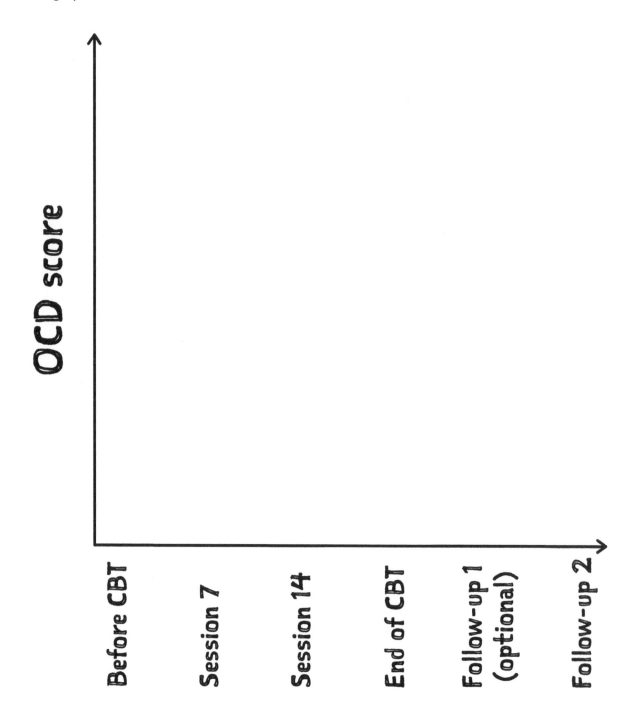

FOLLOW-UP 3

FOLLOW-UP 3 PLAN

- Review and plan ☐
- Review and measure OCD ☐
- Anything you want to add to the agenda? ☐

. . . .

. . . .

. . . .

. . . .

. . . .

. . . .

. . . .

REVIEW AND PLAN

Let's have a look over what we did last session:

- Did you manage to stick to the plan we came up with? What went well and what was tricky?

  . . . .

  . . . .

- What OCD symptoms have you kept away?

  . . . .

  . . . .

- What parts of OCD have been tricky to manage?

  . . . .

  . . . .

- Let's have a look at your relapse prevention plan from Session 20. Is there anything we need to change on it?

  . . . .

  . . . .

- Let's come up with a plan on how to tackle parts of OCD that are still troubling you. What do you need?

- Is there anything coming up that may make it difficult to do the plan? What can you do to overcome this?

  . . . .

  . . . .

REVIEW AND MEASURE OCD

- You may have found things have got better, worse or stayed the same since your last session.
- Your therapist will take a measure of your OCD in this session. Put your scores on the graph below:

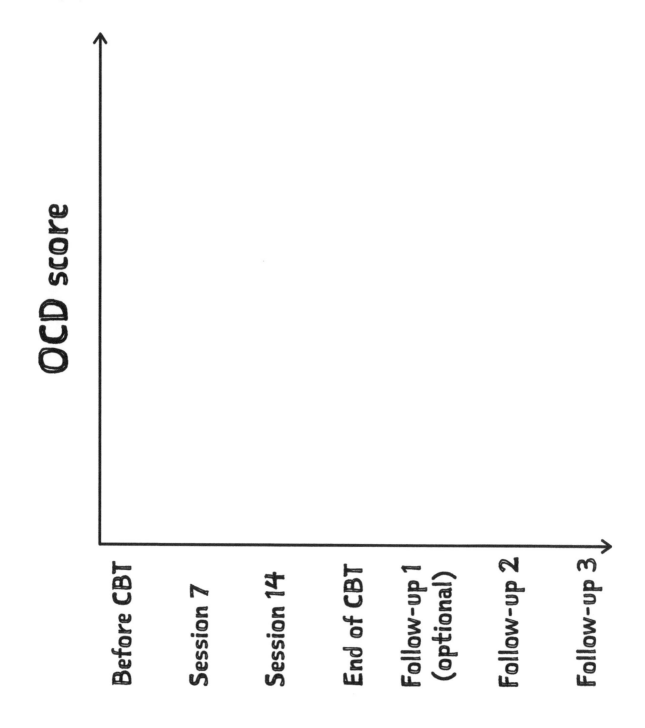

FOLLOW-UP 4

249

FOLLOW-UP 4 PLAN

- Review and plan

- Review and measure OCD

- Looking to the future

- Anything you want to add to the agenda?

. . . .

. . . .

. . . .

. . . .

. . . .

. . . .

. . . .

REVIEW PROGRESS AND PLAN

REVIEW AND PLAN

✏️ Let's have a look over what we did last session:

● Did you manage to stick to the plan we came up with? What went well and what was tricky?

....

....

● What OCD symptoms have you kept away?

....

....

● What parts of OCD have been tricky to manage?

....

....

● Let's have a look at your relapse prevention plan from Session 20. Is there anything we need to change on it?

....

....

● Let's come up with a plan on how to tackle parts of OCD that are still troubling you. What do you need?

● Is there anything coming up that may make it difficult to do the plan? What can you do to overcome this?

....

....

REVIEW AND MEASURE OCD

- You may have found that things have got better, worse or stayed the same since your last session.
- Your therapist will take a measure of your OCD in this session. Put your scores on the graph below:

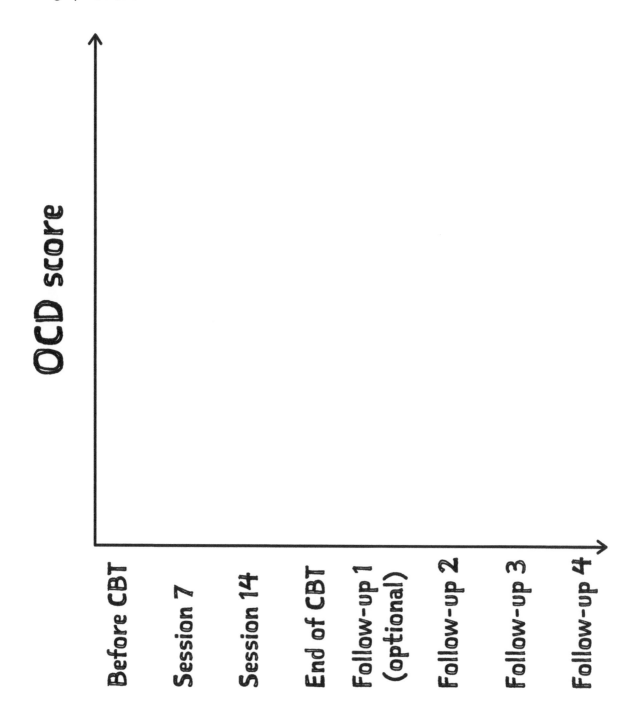

LOOKING TO THE FUTURE

Your treatment sessions and follow-ups have now come to an end. Some people feel scared treatment is ending and some are relieved it's over!

Let's look at the goals you set yourself at the beginning of treatment (Session 5):

- Which goals have you achieved?

  . . . .

  . . . .

- Which ones were tricky to achieve?

  . . . .

  . . . .

  . . . .

- What plan do you have moving forward?

  . . . .

  . . . .

- What are you looking forward to in the future?

  . . . .

  . . . .